Navigating Life's Obstacles

Navigating Life's Obstacles

Dr. Jeffery A Clements

Charleston, SC
www.PalmettoPublishing.com

Navigating Life's Obstacles
Copyright © 2023 by Dr. Jeffery A Clements

First Edition

Hardcover ISBN: 979-8-8229-0689-1
Paperback ISBN: 979-8-8229-0690-7
eBook ISBN: 979-8-8229-0691-4

Table of Contents

Preface

By Dr. Jeffery Austin Clements

This is my life story in vignettes, starting with the strong, well-intentioned attempts of my parents to shield me and my brother from the type of harsh upbringing they had suffered during the Jim Crow era. They never talked about any of the harsh realities of racism that they experienced or what they had to go through to get to where they were in life. Maybe they were uncomfortable or just too busy trying to keep ends meeting to think about it, or maybe it was not important to me then. This protection led me to being somewhat naïve on subtle racial issues here on the West Coast during my upbringing. Despite this, my parents ingrained in us the notion that we could be anything we wanted to be if we worked at it. My father echoed this philosophy throughout my life. Fortunately, it eventually instilled in me an unrelenting self-confidence amid many of my pursuits later in life.

I experienced many obstacles that just about took me out and I retained them as profound lessons learned. These ranged from life-or-death situations on the one hand to earning a doctorate in engineering and getting nominated for National Black Engineer of the Year. I was catapulted out of my sheltered life mainly because of two major life-changing events—a Black history class eye-opener and a surprise, unplanned church speech. These events forcefully compelled me to become a more assertive person with insightful points of view. There are numerous crazy events that I have chosen to include and not hide. The discussion of racially motivated experiences in my life is inevitable, yet that is not the theme of this autobiography.

My life story is presented in vignettes, in approximate chronology, featuring my noteworthy and important events. Within these eighteen chapters are success stories, failures, heartbreaks, setbacks, breakthroughs, skeletons, dirt, triumphs, hilarious moments, and more.

I believe the African American population has not substantially grown. I believe attempts should be made to preserve this phenomenally resilient race of people. I have only two children and three grandchildren to make my contribution to the Black race. My father, Walter, his parents, and all six of his siblings have left this life. He would have been over one hundred years old now, but he only lived eighty-eight years. My mother, Dorothy, her parents, and all seven of her siblings have also transitioned. She passed at ninety-six years old. I am the eldest survivor of the Walter Clements family ancestry line. Despite our shortcomings and flaws, my generation has provided strong shoulders to stand on for the next generation and sent the elevator down for them to advance and prosper.

As a moderately accomplished Black man of seventy-eight years, I stumbled through the "White experience" in America as a Black person. Mine was no easy path to success, often riddled with unimagined obstacles that almost hampered even my basic existence, let alone my striving for any success. As I started to recall the details of events of my life that took place many years ago the bits and pieces seemed to emerge, allowing me to reconstruct more detailed accountings of things I had not thought about for many years. It was like filling in the blanks. For example, when I set our family house on fire as a toddler—I distinctly recall lighting the pretty, red-tipped sticks and innocently flinging them to the floor. As I started immersing myself in that memory, a more accurate picture emerged, and I can now admit that I was responsible for burning up our bedroom.

I must admit I have done several shaky things in my life, as you will read, partly due to immaturity at that time. I struggle with revealing some of these to my kids, family, and close friends, but not one of us is perfect, and everyone has flaws; many of us choose to keep these to ourselves. My slate will be clean after this autobiography (for better or worse). I did not invent anything like the wheel, the automobile, or the mouse trap, but within my accomplishments, I have a few things to boast about. I am not ashamed to share that one of my greatest personal feats was graduating with a trifling 2.000 grade point average from Long Beach State College (LBSC) but then turning things around to earn a PhD in engineering from the UCLA School of Engineering.

It bothers me to this day that, like many Black men, I felt compelled to be an excellent representative of Black people in any situation or in any endeavor I undertook. My professional life was marked with the mindset to attempt to look the (W)right way while in the presence of my White colleagues. This included respecting their rules of appropriate attire, polite demeanor, or just speaking like White people. I do not know how many times my brilliant officemate Phil Grote, who was White, pointed out how he could tell immediately if I was talking on the phone to one of my Black buddies or to a White person. "Hey, man—what's happening?" Many things that have haunted me for most of my life are revealed herein for the first time, before I forget or transition.

Chapter I
Parents' Roots

Colored Parents

My father, Walter Clements II, lived with his parents (Walter I and Mary) and six siblings in the Delta of Water Valley, Mississippi, where they toiled as sharecroppers. Their cabin did not have electricity, running water, or a toilet. They labored in their personal farmyard raising chickens and vegetables. They worked in a White man's cotton fields on the Delta picking cotton under the control of White supremacy from sunup to sundown. Their goal was to produce as many bales of cotton as possible to pay for food, clothing, tools, lodging, and the fee paid to the White man for allowing them to work the land. Each year they would do their accounting with the plantation owner to determine the net differences between earnings and expenses. This was called "settling up." Every year Grandfather Walter realized he was getting deeper and deeper into debt. He saw the writing on the wall with no question—they needed to get out of the situation. They mustered the fortitude to sever the bonds of that dead-end life, to escape to opportunities elsewhere.

My father was about six years old, and his father, mother, and siblings developed their getaway strategy. The consequences of failure

Jeff's rendition of grandparents' sharecropper escape

could be devastating for the entire family. The sun had set, and my grandfather carefully surveyed the area around their cabin. He looked in the distance and saw there was no one near the big house milling around to watch them. He signaled to my father to bring the mule wagon carriage around front. His other sons went inside the cabin and got their mother. They threw all their belongings onto the wagon, left fifty dollars to cover some of their debts, and quietly slipped down the road and through the woods. When the family was a safer distance away, my young father steered the mule-driven wagon at times. They successfully slipped away from the farm, fearing all the while the landlord might hear them and force them to return.

Miraculously, they were not caught. They navigated their way across state lines to Millington, Tennessee, where they all stayed with my grandfather's older brother Wayne who had already taken up residence in Millington (see Attachment 1: Family Tree).

Boarding School

Years later, in Millington, my father went to Woodstock Boarding School, where students had academic classes and performed all necessary chores, including gardening, cooking, cleaning, and laundering. African American students from elementary schools within a thirty-mile radius of Woodstock were bused to the boarding school to finish their high school education.

Under Mr. Roddy's principalship, the school became recognized for its strict high school course guidelines. Boys planted and tended gardens and fields, which provided food for students and faculty members who lived in the wooden dorms. Girls put their domestic science skills to use in cooking and sewing. The White farmers came to the school to take some of the students to work on their farms. My father continued his schooling and worked in the cotton fields to earn a living and save money. He was able to secure the job of lighting the school furnace every day.

My father met my mother at Woodstock, where she had come to school when she, along with her parents and seven siblings, moved to Millington from Arlington, Tennessee. My mother was very light-skinned and could "pass for White." On the other hand, my dad was blessed with an abundance of pigment and had masculine features. My father was rambunctious and took a liking to my mother. She was very beautiful, petite, and well mannered. Mr. Roddy did not think too much of my father and tried to discourage him from courting my mother. My father took up welding classes at the school in hopes of getting a good job earning good money to convince my mother of better days ahead. He had heard there were lots of jobs in the ship building industry in California.

Mr. Roddy, as principal of the school, was not encouraging to many of the boys there, frequently calling them 'stupid' to their faces. Perhaps he was trying to toughen them up. He seemed quite mean and remained principal long after his useful time. It was not until years later that the boarding school developed a comprehensive curriculum to offer a high school diploma. In 1965, London Stevenson, a family friend, became the first Woodstock graduate to enroll in a military academy and eventually became a court judge in California.

Chapter 2

Dad Escaped Sharecropping

Best Cotton Picker in Town

My father said he got "so good" at picking cotton that he became the best cotton picker in the area. However, the limited opportunities in Millington forced him to think he might never be able to leave the area, though he wanted so badly to try his luck in California. He had a dream of becoming successful in California. My father discussed this with my mom, and she encouraged him to take the chance if he really felt he could make it. He was smart, was very ambitious, and trusted himself. He and my mother got married, and he promised he would get to California and earn enough money to send for her. His older brother Wayne decided to help him out by mortgaging one of his cows for seventy-five dollars. This, along with Dad's savings, provided him enough money to travel by train to San Pedro, California.

Sharecroppers working the fields

Travel to California

On the train to California, my father managed to get a job washing dishes. Menial jobs were easy to secure at that time, and he felt confident he would be able to get some work if he hustled a little. When he arrived in the seaport city of San Pedro, he walked around to check out the area and managed to find and purchase an old, dilapidated car. He slept in it for almost a year while working at Todd's Shipyard as a welder. He was ambitious, and even though San Pedro was home to the infamous area known as Beacon Street, known for gambling, fast women, and other enticements, he stayed the course of working and saving money.

Making It Work in San Pedro

After a year my father and two of his buddies, Mac and Otis, also from Tennessee, managed to get and share a one-room apartment. There was only one bed, so they arranged to sleep in it in three different eight-hour shifts. This allowed one to enter the rented bedroom, tap the other on the head, and ask him to get up to relinquish his spot in the bed. The times were tough, but because they shared their resources, they were able to accomplish more, and they remained the closest of friends the rest of their lives.

Chapter 3

Seaport Town Upbringing

Sent for My Mother

After working in the shipyard for almost a year, my father finally saved enough money to send for his wife. She arrived after a few months. In the meantime he found some affordable housing in San Pedro in an area called Banning Homes—a one-bedroom unit. It was a shotgun-style house with a small kitchen, a small living room, one bathroom, and one small bedroom. You could open the front door and see all the way through the house to the back door. There were three other units similar to this one attached to each other.

Fire in Banning Homes

A few years later, when I was about three years old, I nearly burnt down our house in Banning Homes. That particular night is still vivid in my memory. My younger brother, Walter, was in a crib at the foot of my bed. I was privileged to sleep on the big bed in our one-bedroom row house. My mother was in the kitchen cooking and cleaning. My father was at work. I don't know where or what his job was at that time.

Right next to the bed on a makeshift nightstand were a bunch of items, including a box. I remember picking up the box and managing to slide it open to see all the red-tipped stick things inside. I took one out and fiddled with it and probably accidentally scratched the rough brown side. After several scrapes, to my amazement, the stick began to fizzle, glow, and burn. This was amazing to my evolving scientific mind. Wow! With no idea of what fire could do, I was excited. While continuing to lie on my back, I flicked the burning match to my right side onto the floor so I could try this amazing feat again. I removed another "stick" from the box and was again successful in striking and lighting. This was really cool. I repeated this toy exercise several more times. I noticed something yellow emerging from where I had thrown the sticks. I continued to lie there glancing over at the commotion. Suddenly my mother let out a loud scream, ran over, and grabbed me and, from his crib, Walt. She put us in the front yard of the little shotgun house. I could see her filling a big pot of water from the sink. I became worried and scared, although I was fascinated by all the commotion. The fire continued to expand, and she was unsuccessful in putting it out. I only remember that after some time people were gathered outside. A man soon came up the walkway dressed in what looked to me to be funny-looking baggy clothes with a big helmet. He was dragging a hose and began shooting water into the very room where I had been.

Later I saw my father calmly walking down the sidewalk. He did not say anything to me, though he usually greeted us. He walked over to my arms-flailing mother, and they talked. That evening I got to peek into the house to see the blackened room and family

Fire in the bedroom

items strewn across the floors. I was too young to feel sorry or guilty but was only curious about all the activity from the fire department and neighbors all standing around. I do not remember being punished or even being scolded by my parents. Still, we had to move. To this day I am not sure if that house was eventually restored.

We stayed in Banning Homes for several years. We made friends with some of the kids whose parents worked at the shipyard. Some of our friends' parents had migrated from Tennessee with my father, like Mac and Otis. Each had moved from Millington to San Pedro and had begun raising kids. Our new place in Banning Homes was a single-standing bungalow that was grouped with five identical cottages. There were perhaps fifty or so such cottage clusters of six in the large complex. Streets interconnected all of them. When my father came home from the shipyard, my brother and I would often greet him and race him down the sidewalk to our front door. He never beat us. We believed we were the fastest kids in the neighborhood. This likely led to my future confidence and success in track and field.

One thing we enjoyed doing was watching movies at the drive-in theater, which was only a few blocks from our house. A group of about eight of us figured out how to watch the movies for free. There was a long hill alongside the theater where we could see the screen at a slight angle. The only problem was, no sound. We figured out a way around this. One of us would climb the fence and walk over to two of the unused speaker posts and turn it up to the maximum volume. We could hear it from the hill and watch the movie and cartoons. Those were some of the good old days; they lasted until I was about seven years old, when we moved to Black Hills.

Chapter 4

Free-Roaming Childhood

Protected My Little Brother

Our new house was in a neighborhood called Black Hills, located at the very end of what is now the 110 Harbor Freeway. It was a lower-middle-class neighborhood on a hill overlooking Todd's Shipyard. Walter and I had an insatiable appetite to explore and an inherent curiosity about things. It was a time when the milkman delivered milk to our house door. There were only black-and-white TVs with no remote controls, and we watched *Zorro*, *Crusader Rabbit*, and *Amos 'n' Andy*. Burgers were fifteen cents. Our best friends were Stanley and Richard; both were Mexican American. The Barton Hill Elementary School was only a few blocks away. When we first moved there, we had free rein to roam throughout the neighborhood from sunrise to sunset. Our old house, a little bigger than it was originally, remains there to this day. We have tenants staying there now.

We attended Barton Hill Elementary School and would walk to school daily. As we walked, we joined other kids walking to school. The school was quite racially diverse and had few problems. One day some of my friends approached me, telling me some other kids had hit and hurt my little brother. I was not a fighter or a bully, but I did go to where the kids were located and asked which one of the five had hit my little brother. They pointed to one kid who was the tough leader of the group. I simply walked up to him and punched him in the stomach. He buckled over and started to cry. We were too young to have gangs during this era. I just walked away and never thought any more about it. I did not feel tough or like a bad dude. It simply seemed like the right thing to do.

Early Jobs and Unwanted Pet

In 1950, when I was about seven years old, I began working various jobs around my Black Hills neighborhood. I joined a group to clean bricks from a demolished brick building for ten cents a brick. Later I worked at W. T. Grant's clothing store opening boxes and sorting the packages inside.

I eventually got a job, when I was about ten, as a paperboy delivering the *San Pedro News-Pilot* newspaper. I was proud of my job, and my parents were equally proud. The newspaper company would deliver the unfolded papers to me, and I would fold each into a five-by-five thin square that could be tossed. I got pretty good at tossing it into yards and was able to land it on the porches as far as thirty feet away. A few times I hit a hanging planter but biked away acting like I had not noticed.

One day, during my paper route, I threw my paper toward one of my customer's houses, and it landed near some bushes. I walked toward the paper to place it better and noticed something squirming away. Looking closer, I noticed a beautifully colored garter snake scrambling to get back into the bushes. I reacted and grabbed the two-foot snake before it could get away and watched it wiggle and squirm. I was so excited and looked forward to sharing it with my father. If I had known he was deathly afraid of snakes, I would have presented it differently.

In any case I put the snake in my paper-route bag, and it comfortably slithered into my bag. I was excited and rushed home when I finished my route. My mother was in the kitchen, and I told her I had found a new pet I wanted to show Daddy. She did not pay me much attention and kept cooking, so I went into the den where my dad was sitting in his chair in the corner, focused on the basketball game. I reached into the bag, pulled out the snake, and said, "Look, Daddy, what I found today." He did not pay much attention and merely nodded but stayed focused on the game. I approached him more closely and put the snake a few inches from his face. Now, when my father, who was a serious, strong, and dignified man who never overreacted to anything, saw the wiggling snake inches from his face, he appeared to levitate into the air while maintaining a seated position. His eyes and mouth flew open as he made a high-pitched squeal. He yelled, "Boy, get that thing away from me!" Instead of him being happy to see my new pet snake, he was terrified. He yelled at me and told me to get that thing out of this house and take it to the park and kill it. Both scared and sad, I took it to the park, but I did not kill it.

Early Baptism

I was one of the first kids to get baptized at our local place of worship, Mount Sinai Missionary Baptist Church. I was about seven years old. I remember Reverend Coffield having me walk down the steps and into the water located in a big bathtub pulpit in the front of the church. He and I both had on white gowns. He asked me if I believed in God and if I accepted Jesus as my Lord and Savior. I said yes. He told me to hold my breath, and he dunked me under the water. That was it. There were only about five people watching, with no music, and no one clapped.

Afterward my mother took me and my brother to church at Mount Sinai for Sunday school almost every Sunday. We had little booklets we were supposed to take home to read and be prepared to discuss next Sunday. Nobody forced us to read them, so we didn't. We had lots of friends to play with at the church, and several of them were quite naughty boys. We would run around outside playing with each other and often bought some candy from Deacon Glosson, who would line the candy up neatly in the trunk of his car. We did not necessary look forward to going over the Bible lessons in class but did look forward to playing with our friends and buying Deacon Glosson's penny candy.

Indecent Hayride

Each year Mount Sinai would host several group events, including annual picnics. When I was about twelve years old, I remember going on one of the church's hayride trips to a local park. There were about ten kids squeezed together on the back of an open wagon with bales of hay and straw strewn all over. It was a mixed company of boys and girls, including one particular girl I was fond of. I sat next to my mischievous friend Harry.

After we had been riding for a while, he leaned over to me and asked me to smell his index finger. I looked at him as if he were crazy. He whispered, "Come on, Jeff, just take a quick smell." I said, "No way." He moved his finger toward my face and said, "Just tell me what you think it smells like." I took a quick whiff and looked at him. It had a strange odor that I had never smelled before, but it seemed fascinating. He asked me again, "What do you think?" I didn't know. I noticed he was sitting very close to the girl I had a slight crush on and considered very beautiful, although she was perched above us, straddling two hay bales. Harry was slightly below her. He looked over at me and took his other hand and pinched his thumb and forefinger together, forming a little donut circle. He then took his smelly index finger and poked it into the little hole he had just created. He poked it through a few times. He had this sinister grin, but I did not get was he was doing at first. I then looked around at his position under the straddling girl and started putting things together. My feelings were wounded, and I called him a nasty dog, grimaced, and quickly moved away from him, but down deep I think I was a little bit jealous.

I began to question my own level of maturity and exposure to intimate behaviors. Keep in mind sexual-related issues during my era were much more conservative compared to our much more liberal, loose values and behaviors nowadays. Were these types of interactions taking place all around me all the time? Was I just too naïve from leading a relatively sheltered life? I didn't know then, nor do I know the answer to those questions now.

A Stolen Penny

There were two small corner grocery stores in our Black Hills neighborhood. One of them we call Joe's, and the other one, which was only about a block and a half from our house, we called Alvarado's store. We started frequenting them when we were about seven years old. We would stop at Alvarado's to buy candy when we were out playing, and sometimes our parents sent us to the store to buy certain food items. We were honest kids and had a good rapport with Alvarado. We would walk there, get the items, and walk back home.

One day, when I was about nine years old, my father gave me money to buy bread. The small store had two short aisles stocked primarily with food items, including some refrigerated items. Alvarado manned the store alone. I went in and looked around and picked out Wonder Bread. At that time, bread was only about thirty-three cents for a loaf. My dad had given me fifty cents. As I went to the counter, I saw there was some bubble gum there for only one penny, just one cent. Surely my father would not notice a missing penny. I gave Alvarado fifty cents, two quarters, and he charged me thirty-three cents for the bread and one penny for the bubble gum, so he gave me back sixteen cents instead of seventeen cents. Clearly, to me, a penny was trivial and insignificant.

I headed back home with the bread in my hand and the gum in my pocket. If I had known then the ruckus this would create, I would have skipped the gum. Just the two of us were home at the time. I handed Dad the bread and sixteen cents in change. He suspiciously asked how much the bread was. I said thirty-three cents. He looked at me and asked whether this was all the change Alvarado had given me because I should have gotten seventeen cents back. I hesitated and said yes, not telling him about the gum in my pocket. I could see the anger brewing on his face, and I was not about to say anymore. The more he thought about it, the more furious he became. "That Alvarado cheated you out of one penny." I didn't explain anything to him, and he said, "We're going to go right back up to Alvarado's store, and I'm going to tell him that he's just cheated my son, and he's probably been cheating us all the time."

So we marched back up the street to the store, with him firmly holding my hand. My father stormed into the store and started giving Alvarado a tongue-lashing you would not believe. He told Alvarado some things he probably had never heard before. "You've been cheating my kids out of a penny, thinking I wouldn't notice." Alvarado looked at him with astonishment, knowing that I had spent one extra penny. I was absolutely trembling, certain my days on this earth were over, but for some reason, Alvarado did not tell on me and gave my dad the missing penny. Dad and I walked home from there, and I was terrified and worried that he would find out that Alvarado did not cheat us but rather that I stole a penny. I never had the courage to tell my father what happened, and it has bothered me throughout my life. Even when he was in his last days, I thought about it but could not muster the strength to tell him what really happened. The simple incident is something I never got over, and it still haunts me.

Ship's Anchor Chain

A few years after the snake paper-route issue, by the time I was about ten years old, my brother, Walter, and I were quite independent and very mischievous. We would leave in the morning and return home in the evening without any trouble. We had no cell phones or other ways of communicating with our parents while away. There were a few phone booths sparsely scattered throughout the neighborhood.

Often a bunch of us would ramble down to Todd's Shipyard and walk past the gates to goof around. I was the de facto leader. Todd's Shipyard is now referred to as the Port of Los Angeles. At that time giant ships were docked there. This was well before the appearance of the giant cranes and railroad boxcars being loaded onto and off the ships. My brother and about six other boys roamed the fields where the ships' anchors were positioned near the shore. I think I was the oldest. Somehow, we made our way over to the base of the giant anchor coming from the ship. I looked at the giant chain links, each nearly as long as we were, and thought that if we could climb up, we could see what was on the ship. We went over to the first link we could reach and climbed up onto it. I convinced the others to follow me because I was going to climb all the way up to the ship. (I now guess it was more than a hundred feet). As I climbed, they all followed me. After a while we found ourselves over the water and very high up, somewhere between the ship and the dock, and I finally realized my situation. I had been hanging upside down with my arms and legs wrapped around a chain link; I was very tired. I could have fallen into the murky water below. I realized I could barely swim and I could not make it all the way to the ship. If we all fell into the water, we might all drown.

I yelled back, telling all those precariously suspended to move backward and go back. At first they did not get the memo. My grip began to weaken, so I yelled again, this time with unmistakable anger and fright. Nobody objected, and we began the long, slow descent while hanging upside down from about thirty feet above the

Climbing ship anchor chain

water. With extreme fatigue we all made it safely back to the dock. We would never tell our parents about this escapade. I must admit that was the most dangerous thing I ever did as a kid.

Girl Rejection Fears

Early in the 1950s, when I was about eleven years old, I was infatuated with Mary Jo. I thought she was very pretty and nice. I was too shy to approach her, but my buddies tried to convince me she would not bite.

One afternoon my buddies and I decided to go to the Warner Brothers theater to watch a movie and cartoons. It was about two miles from our houses. Someone suggested we pass by Mary Jo's house and ask if she would like to walk with us. We walked by her house and they insisted that I go to her upstairs apartment and ask if she wanted to join us. She opened the door and we talked. She said OK but had to ask her mom. Her mom looked out of the window and down at the two girls and three boys waiting, and she said OK.

We headed to the movies with Mary Jo and me leading the pack. We arrived, and I paid twenty-five cents for her ticket and mine. We sat in seats next to each other. The other five kids of the entourage decided to sit directly behind us. As the movie proceeded, I struggled to figure out how to tell her I liked her. I was very nervous but remained motionless. Suddenly I was startled as my entourage, from behind, lifted my right arm to place it around Mary Jo.

Theater

At first I was annoyed but soon gave in as they began creating a racket. There stayed my arm—cold and stiff—for the remainder of the movie. I was too fearful to say "I like you" while at the movies, and afterward we headed back to our homes. When we got to her apartment, they urged and pushed me to escort her upstairs. They all waited downstairs to see what I was going to do. I was absolutely petrified, knowing what I wanted to say but not able to get it out. As she opened her door, she turned around and she just looked at me. I mustered all the strength in my being to lean forward to peck her on the lips. She gave me a polite hug and went inside, and as she began closing the door, I said, "Thank you." My face lit up like sparkles. I was on cloud nine, and I felt I was the great Casanova. I was in heaven and could not hold back shrieking with joy.

I looked downstairs at the entourage grinning, snickering, and high fiving. Something had gotten ahold of me, and exuberance took over. I leaped from the top of the stairs to the bottom, almost crippling my ankles. This was a happy day for all of us. Mary Jo and I never became an actual couple but were close friends for a while.

BB Gun Incident

I had only minor injuries in my life. I suffered a broken right wrist in elementary school while playing football and later a sliced wrist from Brenda. I was extremely lucky a few other times. In 1958 my father had a Daisy BB gun in the house. One day my brother was playing with the BB gun outside. We had not loaded it with any BBs, but he did not realize there was one BB still in the chamber. He figured out how to pump the handle to power the rifle and started aiming it around at various objects. One of the random aims was at me, and he pulled the trigger. A BB flew out and hit me in my right eye. Fortunately, I had prescription glasses on at that time, but the BB shattered the brittle glass, and shards went directly into my right eye. For some strange reason, I instantly knew not to blink, or I would shred my eye, so I kept it closed.

We ran into the house and told my mother. She knew it was an emergency. We jumped into the car and raced to the Harbor General Hospital emergency room. They assessed the situation and flushed all the glass out of my eye, while I never blinked once. I don't know how I managed this, but God is good. I was relieved, and the only thing I needed was a new pair of glasses, but there is a red spot on my sclera to this day.

A few more health and medical problems occurred, but the most dreaded one, later in life, was cancer.

Near School Expulsion

Around 1957 I began attending Richard Henry Dana Junior High School, which was about three and a half miles from our house. We would leave in the morning, and often many friends would join us on the way to school. By the time we got there, there would be about ten to fifteen of us converging on Dana Junior High, boisterous and together.

One day, when I was in the ninth grade, my curiosity got me into big trouble. It was lunch break, and my friend and I were walking around the various buildings doing nothing. As we walked, I noticed the fire alarm mounted to one of the buildings seemed to be damaged; at least something was wrong with the cover. I stopped to examine it a little more closely and could see some of its inner workings. I wondered how it actually worked. My friend saw me examining it and yelled at me not to fool around with it. I listened to him, but as we were about to leave, I became curious about the little flap that seemed to be just dangling there. My curiosity got the best of me. I really wanted to just touch it, so I did; nothing happened immediately, and we just walked away.

After we had walked about ten feet away, all hell broke loose. Every alarm on every building and structure went off. We panicked and could only think to follow what they had drilled into all the students in the case of such events—go to the big open blacktopped area. So we did. Every student and faculty member headed down to the blacktopped areas. All the administrative offices emptied. The cafeteria staff and everyone else were there. I would guess there were several hundred people. I went to my designated place in a line and waited. Trembling with absolute fear, I wondered if I had caused this, if anyone had seen me, and if I should say something about how this had been an accident.

We all stood there in the field for about an hour, until bells began to ring and instructions came down that we could go back to our class because it was a false alarm. I made it back to my class and sat in my seat. About fifteen minutes after I returned, the class bungalow door opened and the principal of the school, the vice principal, some other staff members, and a little girl entered the class. They all stood at the door for a few minutes scanning the class. The girl looked around the room and finally spotted me and yelled,

"There he is!" I was so terrified I wanted to bolt from the classroom if I could. They escorted me down to the principal's office. While there I had the fleeting thought that the Black vice principal was about to leap across the room to start beating me. He said that type of disrespect and disregard for rules should lead to school expulsion. I had never thought of myself as the type who would be expelled from school. I was absolutely terrified. After the principal, vice principal, and staff consulted in another room for a while, they returned. They had reviewed my record and could see my terrified face. They talked to me for a while as I boohooed, and they accepted it was a curiosity accident and warned me not to do anything like that ever again. I don't think they ever told my parents, and they did not have to tell me twice.

Chapter 5

Multitasking Parents

Mom Worked Day Jobs

My mother worked jobs cleaning houses in Palos Verdes for ten dollars per client during the 1960s. Being a house cleaning lady was not a demeaning job at that time, and I never thought it was below her dignity. She was also able to get hired in at the Van Camp's tuna factory on Terminal Island. The hourly rate was much better than that of most other labor jobs. She eventually went to school and became a nurse's aide at Harbor General Hospital. She was well liked there, really enjoyed her job, and had pride. Because of her relatively light skin, she was privy to many White conversations and situations, until people saw my well-pigmented father. She said the only time she really had a scare was when she was in the morgue room of the hospital with the deceased and she thought she saw one of the bodies move. She moved with

Mom

lightning speed out of the room and refused any related assignments in that area thereafter.

My parents talked very little about their upbringing in Tennessee. My mother especially did not think it was appropriate to bring up disturbing events of their pasts. I remember when my father was telling my brother and me about his aunt who was working for a White man in Tennessee. He recalled when she pointed out how some of the man's buddies would come over when she was cleaning the house, each forcing themselves upon her. My mother would quickly intervene and scold my father for bringing up those events with us. We almost never got to hear about any of the really tragic stories he experienced.

Mom maintained a very immaculate house. Nothing remained out of place for long. My father was the one most often guilty of leaving things out of order. It turned out I retained these tidiness qualities. I notice untidy things at home, at work, and at other people's homes. This has sometimes caused problems. One problem this obsessive tidiness quality created is that family members often tease me about the arrangement of food on my plate. I have an awkward habit of always arranging the various food items on my plate to not touch each other. I do it now without thinking, and it is a habit I have not been able to break.

Dad's Employment at Steel Mill

In 1960, while I was in Dana Junior High and thirteen years old, my father worked several jobs, including owning his own car wash business. He had his own small facility with materials and supplies. My younger brother, Walt Jr., and I would sometimes sit in the little windowless one-room structure with an attached port area, eating our favorite snack, which consisted of a Twinkie wrapped with a slice of baloney (how we said "bologna" in those days). This was our lunch prior to starting to work with our father. He had developed superior forearm strength and muscles from washing the cars. My father was kind and friendly, always with a smile on his face, so he easily developed a loyal customer base consisting of well-to-do Palos Verdes residents. One thing I never questioned was why he frequently greeted us endearingly by saying, "Here come the jiggaboos." He used this as a welcoming ingratiating phrase over his lifetime. It was not until recently I found out it had a very derogatory racial meaning. I am not sure if I would have tried to point out the negative meaning to him. He thought it was cute and funny.

In any case he was very social and wise, and people would always listen to his opinions. His full-time job was with Columbia Steel in Torrance, California. He was proud to work there, had a strong work ethic, and moved up the organizational ladder over time. He was a dedicated, conscientious worker. Even though he moved up in the company, he reached their "glass ceiling" for Black men, stopping him from elevating to a position to supervise any White person. This bothered him, but he only talked about it a few times that I know of.

Adventure in the Toolshed

Little Walter and I had many adventures around the neighborhood, and a major one took place right next door to our home. This was something Walter and I will never forget. We played a lot with Brenda, who lived near us. My brother and I would go to the park that was adjacent to her house and walk around looking at the wildlife and trees and exploring the many trails in the wooded area.

Her backyard was near the park, and we would often leave the park and venture there. Her parents had a little garden with tools and a toolshed. I was a very inquisitive boy, but Brenda was even more inquisitive than I was. She was younger than I but much like a tomboy to me. However, all that changed one afternoon when we were playing in the backyard. Somehow we got on the subject of sex and the difference between boys and girls. She had one sister, and I had one brother. She bragged she knew a lot about sex. I said rather than talk about it, she should show me her stuff. She said OK. That sounded very intriguing to me and my brother. I asked where she would show us her stuff. She said right there: "You let me see yours, and I'll let you see mine."

I said, "No way, not out here in the open."

She said, "OK, let's go right in here."

She pointed to the small toolshed next to us, which was about three feet by four feet and stocked with shovels, rakes, hoes, and other things. So we climbed inside the toolshed, stepping over some of the rakes and shovels, and closed the door.

She said, "OK, I'll show you mine."

I was very interested and became aroused and pulled down my pants. The next thing I knew, we were attempting to have penetration while standing and succeeded in a very awkward manner. I was twelve years old, and I guess you could say I was no longer a virgin after that encounter. Anyway, we went outside, and it was my brother's turn to come in and explore. Later we all departed and went our separate ways. Walt and I went back home.

A day or two later, my mother called both Walter and me into the kitchen area to ask us some questions. She focused on Walter and asked him what he and Brenda had done in the tool-shed. He fumbled and really could not explain what he had done. So my mother asked him directly, "Did you actually put your penis inside of her?" I was listening and stunned as to why she would ask a stupid question like that. I had never heard the word "penis," and I thought she was trying to say "peanut." She asked Walter again, "Did you put your penis inside of her?" I thought, *What kind of ritual would involve putting a peanut inside her?*

I am not sure if Walter ever understood exactly what she was asking. He kind of described what we did, and we were told not to do that again. I was a little angry when he used the word "we" since my mother did not initially include me in the matter. I suppose she told my father, but he never mentioned it to us, and the subject never came up again. I soon found out the difference between a penis and a peanut.

Street Fight with Neighbor

A year or so later, I had a completely different encounter with my neighborhood buddy and tomboy Brenda. She was talking with several of our junior high school friends just across the street from my house. I saw them and decided to wander over to join them. Brenda must have been talking about something a little private and did not want me to hear. I entered the conversation, just as I always did. She told me I needed to go back home. I asked why. When she said, "Because I said so," it angered me quite a bit, but that was how she rolled sometimes. I saw several of my friends, and they egged me on by challenging me. "Are you going to let her tell you what to do?" I said no and walked toward her. She was standing near the edge of the sidewalk, almost leaning against a parked car. She again told me to go back home. I again refused. She reached down and grabbed the drinking end of an empty Coca-Cola bottle lying on the grass. I stood there holding my ground. She then took the bottle and smashed it on the curb, leaving the narrow drinking end in her hand and the jagged razor-sharp pieces on the other end. She was only about a few inches from me. I stood there shocked and motionless, mainly because I was too close to back away or run. She quickly took the jagged broken edge of the bottle and swiped my left wrist. I looked down at a one-and-a-half-inch-long gash. The thought raced through my mind that this tomboy was also about to jab me in the stomach. Instinctively my right fist slammed into the left side of her head. She fell back onto the parked car, possibly semiconscious. She went down, and I scampered back across the street and showed the large gash to my mom. She was both angry and greatly concerned. Since she was a nurse's aide, she knew how to clean it and apply gauze and bandages. That seemed sufficient to stop the bleeding for the moment, and we did not need to dash to the hospital to get stitches.

A week or so later, she talked to Brenda's mother to understand and resolve what had happened. Several weeks later I finally saw her: her left eye was still completely closed, and her face was black on the left side. My wrist was healing under that large bandage. However, there remains a one-inch scar to this day. We eventually became friends again and resumed our mischievous ways. I never found out what they were talking about.

Attempted Robbery

One thing that took place while we were still junior-high students shames me most of all. It haunts me to this day. I have never told anybody about this criminal act. The neighborhood girl Brenda, my brother, Walt, and I were walking near Barton Hill Elementary School, heading to the Warner Brothers Theater, where, again, admission cost twenty-five cents. As we walked, the neighborhood girl came up with an idea. If we saw an elderly man, she would get his attention and flirt with him, and Walt and I would walk up behind him and take his wallet from his back pocket. This was absurd and against our basic values. Surprisingly we saw an elderly White man walking toward us. The three of us neophyte criminals glanced at each other and nodded our heads, thinking our plan was being handed to us. She began to get his attention. We walked up behind him and saw his back pocket was buttoned. We thought for a moment, then chickened out, and all three of us dashed away. Later we realized that our plan was pure robbery no matter how you looked at it. All my friends think of me as being very honest and friendly, but that was a dark moment in the past that would have adversely shaped my future. I continue to feel ashamed that I even thought of doing that. Despite our trials, tribulations, and experimentation, Brenda and I were good buddies until she passed away a few years ago. She was a wonderful, wise, and beautiful person who I am proud to have had in my life.

Pet Pigeons

During that same time period of the 1960s, we played around in the neighborhood looking for adventures to undertake. We would watch the many animal species living in our neighborhood. We would see all kinds of birds, including pigeons. One day we had a cardboard box and managed to capture two pigeons using our world-class hunting and poaching skills. We fed them a little bread and water, and they seemed to do OK. We noticed it had become popular to raise pigeons. Walt and I thought it would be fun to give it a try. We quickly realized we needed to do more than keep them in a simple paper box if they were going to survive. We decided to build a wooden cage. My mother was OK with this endeavor, and our father was noncommittal. We solicited help from some of our neighborhood friends to find some wood, wire, and supplies to make a cage. We finally got the cage built. The adults thought it was a raggedy abomination, but we and our friends thought it was a masterpiece to behold.

For some unknown reason, my father never helped or stopped us on this journey. We eventually acquired several more pigeons through capture, trading with others, and purchase. We owned different pigeon types, including checks, blue bars, fantails, feather feet,

Jeff and Walt's pigeon cage

and others. We fed them bread and seeds. Several kids also began raising pigeons. What was so fascinating to us was finally opening the cage and watching them go out and gather together and then fly around the sky completely free yet staying together. We were so elated when they would all return to the raggedy cage we had built with our own hands. They eventually mated and laid eggs; the eggs hatched, and their babies joined the flying with the parents. Perhaps this is why our dad never asked us to tear down the cage—because he saw how much joy, accomplishment, and pleasure it brought us.

Tears in Church

Mom and Dad did not know the details of all the church activities we were involved in, especially the ones we thought it better to keep to ourselves. The hayride trip was one of them.

Mom and Dad served in many capacities in the church. Dad served as a Sunday school teacher, superintendent of the Sunday school, member of the board of trustees, chairman of the board of deacons, and tenor in the Senior and Jubilee Choirs.

One Sunday I arrived late for the sermon at Mount Sinai Baptist Church. Reverend Stanfield was preaching. There were no more seats in the back of the church where I usually sat so I could leave quickly and sneak around the back to goof off. The usher led me to a seat in the front row right under the pulpit where the preacher could look down directly into my face. I did not want this. I had just started wearing my new hard contact lenses. Soft lenses were not available at that time. The optometrist had instructed me to wear them for four hours at a time to train my eyes to get used to them. As the reverend finally got underway with his sermon, my eyes were becoming irritated. I decided to just sit there and let my eyes adjust to the new lenses, but my eyes began to tear up. The preacher looked down and saw I was tearing. He assumed I was being affected by his condemnation sermon. He became more animated as he saw the tears really flowing. He seemed to be directing his emotional sermon to me only as tears streamed down my face. When he finally ended his sermon and there was a break in the proceedings, I booked out of there and dashed to the restroom to remove those hard lenses as fast as I could! Amen!

The New Church

The church membership continued to grow and so did its activities and organizations. Eventually the church members decided to raise money to build a new church. They created a building fund and were finally able to hire an architect to sketch a new building. The design was phenomenal and well received, so they decided to proceed with the project. First they needed a good project manager. The vote was unanimous. It was my father, Walter Clements, whom they chose to lead the effort. Initially I did not appreciate the monumental job that was, but he took it to heart for over three years. Among other things, they had to get the permits, secure contractors to demolish the old church, excavate the grounds, install pillars, build the foundation, erect the two-story structure, and much more. He had to manage a lot of simultaneously moving parts. He would make his way downtown to several government offices then race back to the church to coordinate the construction crew. The church was completed and is one of the most beautiful structures in San Pedro. There is no son on this earth who is as proud as I was of witnessing my dad successfully complete this monumental project.

Original Mt. Sinai Baptist Church

My only disappointment was they never gave him full recognition for what he had accomplished. I thought they would name the main sanctuary after him or at least the main hall. I don't think he burned any bridges, but he did get into a little scuffle with the minister because the minister gave rework instructions directly to his workers without discussing it with my father. My dad was furious about that because he had developed such a good rapport with the construction workers, but the minister ignored his supervisorial position and gave a direct order to the workers. He let the pastor know in no uncertain terms to not ever do that again. They got into a physical altercation. After completion of the church, the congregation offered all kinds of praise and acknowledgment to the minister and others but little to my father. Perhaps that was a sore spot with the minister that never healed for me. I have trouble getting over my suspicions and resentment.

Dad at Mt. Sinai Baptist Church in construction

Dad continued to be very active in the church but also became politically active in the neighborhood. He sat in meetings and frequently offered his wisdom to the top officials in San Pedro. He became president of the first neighborhood community organization, chairman of the deacon board at Mount Sinai Baptist Church, and superintendent of the Sunday school, as I have mentioned. He was always a thoughtful leader whom everyone loved and respected.

The new Mt. Sinai Baptist Church

Chapter 6
Fame in Sports

High School Track Stars

Back in 1959, when I was about fifteen years old, I graduated from Richard Henry Dana Junior High School and began attending San Pedro High School. Pedro was adjacent to Dana but in a slightly elevated location. It was on a nice campus with attractive, sturdy buildings. My brother, Walter, remained at Dana and developed his own friendships, and we did not see each other as much as we had in the past. Walt grew much more social than I did and made lots of friends throughout San Pedro. Prior to this time, I was the boss between us, but after this period, he became more independent and freer of my rule. For the most part, my new buddies were a little more thuggish than my Dana buddies. For most of my time at Pedro, my buddies would hang out in front of the school entrance area. These were all Black kids from the projects and nearby areas. There were some friendly thugs, some bullies, mostly good athletes, but no scholars.

To Steal or Not to Steal

A few years later, a repulsive event took place that remains seared in my mind to this day. I was on the track team, and all the athletes from each sport were assigned a gym locker that included a rotating dial combination lock. The athletes would change in the open locker room, put their street clothes in their lockers, and head to whichever sport they were involved in—track and field, basketball, baseball, and so forth. One day my buddy Jessy pointed out that some of the athletes would leave their lockers partially unlocked by dialing up two of the three numbers, thus allowing the third number to be turned until the lock clicked and then opened. It then took only one turn to open the lock. This allowed them to undress quickly and get in the open showers fast. Jessy said he could open some of the lockers. I did not quite believe him at first, but he told me to watch him. He tested his theory on a few lockers, and they opened.

I wanted to try. I asked him to stand at the end of the row of lockers to make sure no one was coming. So he did. I started trying several lockers, and *voilà*, one turn and it opened. I noticed the locker I had opened had shoes, a shirt, and pants hanging on a hook inside it. I felt the pants, and they had a wallet in them. I took the wallet and looked through it, but it contained no money. I put it back and closed the locker. For a few seconds, I just sat there thinking about what I had just done. It was robbery. It could have been the wallet of a close friend. The whole room seemed to become enveloped by a darkened shadow. I stood up and told Jessy that we really should not be doing this. So we left, luckily not having gotten caught, and I never tried that criminal stunt again.

Jessy was the type of person who gravitated to things our other buddies showed no interest in. One good thing about Jessy was he became an excellent chess player. He finally convinced me to take it up. He taught me the game, and I would play him often. He would checkmate me all the time. I finally decided to get more serious, and

I began studying chess strategies on the side without telling him. We played for over a year, and I lost every time. He showed no mercy. Finally we were about at the same level, and we had a match at his house. I was ready. We battled for well over an hour, and eureka, I saw the checkmate move. I moved my bishop and said, "Check." Today was mine. Jessy thought for a moment and moved his man and said, "Check." I was blindsided as I had not anticipated his clever move. I stared at the board for a long time and finally conceded in my mind that he was going to win. I am not sure what happened next, but my right hand moved like a flash and scattered the pieces all over the floor. Jessy got more satisfaction from that moment of rage than from winning with a checkmate. Anyway, I played him several more times, never defeating him. Jessy was a year older than me and later on always rode his bike for exercise. He and his wife created a vegetable garden with healthy food. Despite all that, he developed Alzheimer's disease and passed away in September 2022. He had a beautiful family, and they will all miss him, as will I.

Dared to Drink

During the same time, in the 1960s, when I was in the heyday of my early high school track career, some kids were quite jealous. When I was about sixteen years old, I went to a party hosted by my cousin (Bob J.) off Adams Boulevard in Los Angeles. He lived with his father on the second floor in an apartment building. His father was out of town, and Bob had decided to throw a small party. There were about fifteen to twenty people there, including several of my friends and my brother. Several were drinking some hard liquor. I did not drink, mainly because I was a competing athlete at that time. Bob and some others saw I was not drinking and started making fun of me. They implied that I was not a man and was scared to have a little drink. I managed to ignore them initially. But they kept it up as they saw me become more aggravated. Finally, I had had enough. I decided I would show them who was tough. I grabbed a large glass and filled it with bourbon. I looked at them and gulped the bourbon down completely. They were all stunned. I then immediately grabbed a bottle of vodka and filled the same glass with vodka and gulped that down. They all stared at me, but nobody said anything. I just stood there looking defiant with a feeling of accomplishment. Little did I know what was coming.

I walked outside onto the second-floor balcony and stood next to the handrail as I looked over the property. Suddenly there seemed to be a major earthquake. I grabbed the handrail tightly to keep from falling due to the shaking. No one else showed signs that they were experiencing the earthquake. I stumbled toward the end of the long rail to the stairs. I started to walk down, but before I realized it, I was already at the bottom. I got up and started walking around the property, babbling away. Somehow my brother and his friends found me about two hours later in another apartment with two girls who had locked me in their bathroom as I babbled away.

My brother and his friend finally got me home to Pedro, where they tried to sneak me past my father. I don't remember Dad saying anything. The next day, they somehow got me ready for work at my summer job at the fish cannery. I was still very drunk and fell asleep (passed out) on a stack of tuna cans. I remained drunk for about two more days, and I don't remember a thing during that period. They probably should have taken me to the hospital. Maybe they did. I have no recollection. I'm just glad I didn't kill myself.

Put Pedro on the Map

After the summer of 1960, I was fully recovered and back on the practice track. It later turned out my track buddies put San Pedro on the map in Los Angeles for their spectacular athletic achievements. Some of my close buddies, including Junie James, Richard Davis,

Louie Mathews, James Sanders, Reggie Parsons, Vernon Williams, Danny Hook, and Randal Hoxie, were all big stars on the track team. The high school track structure consisted of three categories: the Cs, the Bs, and the As. Even though I was of sort a nerd, I was accepted because of my track and field skills—I could outrun most of them. We all started out in the C division and eventually progressed to the A division where we really excelled and won the league championship. I ultimately became runner-up in the well-publicized Los Angeles City Championships, competing against runners from hundreds of great schools. This put San Pedro on the map. I came in third place in the City Championships with my 49.0 school record in the 440-yard dash, which qualified me for the California State Championships. I was in heaven and on my way to even greater things.

Broke Record

In my last year of varsity track at Pedro, I was at my peak performance. There was a little blurb almost every day in the *San Pedro News-Pilot* about me. When I broke the school record for the 440-yard dash, I was on the front of the sports page with a nice picture. I broke Robert McNerney's twenty-year-old Pedro school record. McNerney was well known throughout all of Pedro as he was the founder and owner of the largest mortuary there, which is still in operation: the one-hundred-twenty-acre Green Hills Mortuary and Memorial Chapel in the basin. I did not know him, nor did my family have any interaction with his businesses.

I had run a forty-nine flat (49.0 seconds), breaking his old school record of 50.2. I received several accolades from my family, teammates, friends, and the newspaper. One day I was at home alone and the doorbell rang. I answered it, and there stood a White man in a suit. I assumed he was trying to sell us something. He asked if I was Jeff Clements. I was a little surprised he knew my name. I replied affirmatively. He told me he was Bob McNerney, and he wanted to congratulate me on breaking his school record. I was really surprised, and I did not even think to thank him. He handed me a personally created beautiful trophy that read "Jeff Clements, San Pedro High School, Quarter Mile, Champion 1961, Presented by Robert McNerney." I did not know what to do or say. I had never seen or heard of anything happening like this before. I did not think to invite him in or even ask any questions. I just stood there completely dumbfounded. He finally said congratulations again and wished me the best of luck in the future, then left. Surprisingly the

New Generation, New Record

San Pedro News-Pilot contacted me about taking a picture with Bob on the track field. It was a very quick photo-op moment. Others talked to him, but we never got the chance to chat because he had to rush back to work. I never saw him or talked to him again.

As I became a little more mature, I wanted to go by his business and at least thank him for the trophy, but I was still too shy and immature to do it. I am certain we would have connected and had the most enjoyable and heartwarming conversation about track and field and our teams. He likely would have been a great mentor and adviser to help me deal with many of the hardships, challenges, and struggles I eventually suffered. My life may have been directed down a slightly different but perhaps more informed path in that scenario. I sincerely regret never having talked to him in more detail after that fateful day in 1961. I broke down in tears in his brother's office when he told me Bob had passed away several years ago. I will cherish the one-of-a-kind trophy he presented to me with all my heart forever and will always regret my immaturity during that time in my life.

Demoralizing History

During the tenth grade, in 1960, I was not particularly motivated to study hard or make any kind of academic impact in high school. Unfortunately, something occurred that left a lasting impact on me, one that carries through to this day.

My formal education began back in 1949, while we still lived in Banning Homes. The school was located on the top of a hill where the 110 Harbor Freeway now ends, as I have explained. That was during a time when we got pretty good at practicing the bomb drills of ducking under desks.

In San Pedro I did not experience the overt Jim Crow racism that my parents faced. They carefully concealed those experiences while they were rearing us. However, the subtle, nearly equally cruel, racism became more obvious to me as I got older. I had never thought much about racism as I had had friends of all races. One day, in my high school history class, it all hit me like a ton of bricks. The teacher talked about the founding of America and touched on slavery and the Negro. The Negro was portrayed as inferior and unintelligent. I was stunned by the way the subject was presented in the textbooks. I slid down in my seat after hearing about the superior Whites and the subclass Negroes. I realized I was different from all the classmates sitting around me. I felt so very inferior.

I don't know how many years it took for me to begin to overcome this inferiority complex about me and my race since so many things after that seemed to reinforce our inferiority. I don't feel inferior any longer, but I feel I am different and have different expertise, qualities, and values than other folks. My father played a big role in allowing me to excel and overcome this inferiority complex, probably because he had grown up in the South during the Jim Crow era. He could see through some of the racist tactics, knowing he could not stop it, but he was smart enough to maneuver through the given system. He focused on never bringing it up and on sheltering me from its ills. He constantly told me I was as good as anybody else and could do anything I wanted to do if I put my mind to it. After years it finally sank in, but that demoralizing episode made me think about the diversity in my culture more closely.

Thirteen As or Bs

One day I got into a discussion about future plans with my good buddy Richard Escobedo., who raised pigeons like I did. He was good in math and said he was going to go to college and asked me whether I had considered it. I was not sure if my grades were good enough, but he told me I only needed thirteen As and/or Bs to get into Long Beach State College (LBSC). (It later changed its name to California State University, Long Beach (CSULB).) Since I didn't have the grades, I figured I could probably go to Harbor Junior College, but he further pushed the point that I had two years to get the thirteen grades, and I already had some good grades from my sports. I thought about it for a moment and considered checking into it. That was the first time anybody had talked about me going to college, and I seriously looked at the possibility and worked hard to achieve it.

When it was time to submit the entrance application, I could see I had a chance. Lo and behold, I was accepted into the only college I applied to—CSULB. My buddies, parents, and friends were amazed that I had made it straight into a four-year college. I received accolades of congratulations from all around the neighborhood. That made me and my parents beam with pride. I became a first-generation college student. Few of my friends had achieved that feat.

Most Outstanding Graduate Athlete

When I graduated from San Pedro High School in the summer of 1962, there was a big deal about the class nominating the graduating class's Most Outstanding Graduate Athlete. This included all sports: football, basketball, baseball, track and field, and more. Both male and female athletes were considered. Someone nominated me; I don't know who. I had been unaware of the intense lobbying behind the scenes for this coveted position, especially from my classmates. A White football-nominated candidate was being pushed by his classmate and his twin sister. To be honest I was not really that interested in the award. The election took place, and with all the ballots in, guess who won? Jeffery Clements. It *was* a big deal, and the *San Pedro News-Pilot* had a big half-page spread: "Jeff Clements Wins the Most Outstanding Graduate Athlete." I was proud, and it bolstered my little cocky attitude at that time. Who else were they going to give the award to?

I have since matured and now sincerely appreciate the award.

Chapter 7
College Ordeals and Hardships Begin

When Is Lunch Period?

After graduating from San Pedro High School in 1962, I should have taken a reconnaissance tour of the CSULB campus because I knew nothing about college or college life and had no idea it was going to be such a long and treacherous journey. The campus atmosphere, size, and building locations and where to go for anything were foreign to me. I did not even know how I was going to get to campus daily. During the registration process, I saw very few Black students. While I was walking around, when I saw a brother, we always shared mutual nods (marking our solidarity), whether we knew each other or not. It was an acknowledgment that we were in this struggle together. This became a universal gesture among Black guys. Once, when I was walking with a White student, I nodded to a passing Black person, and the White student asked if I knew him. I said not at all, and the White guy remained confused. He couldn't possibly realize our needs in their sea of White folk.

The registration process almost took me out. I realized that if one made one wrong step, like getting in the wrong line or turning in incomplete information, one might have to start over or fill out more paperwork. It was truly a learning-by-mistakes endeavor, and I had absolutely no assistance or guidance. Fortunately, I had received a full-tuition scholarship because of sports. It was a $47.50-per-semester scholarship, which was a lot in 1962 for a track athlete.

Later on, I met an informal, mostly Black (some Hispanics) group off campus that eventually helped me navigate many obstacles of campus life. For example, I remember the first day I attended all my classes from 10:00 a.m. to 3:00 p.m. and was very hungry. I asked a passing student when they were going to ring the bell for lunch. He looked at me and shook his head. I did not realize I had to plan lunch within my own schedule. Duh!

Not College Material

After a few weeks, I was getting adjusted to college. One of my classes was history, in which I was not doing well. I received an F on both the first and second tests. While I was sitting in the start of a class amid about fifty students, the professor looked around the room and asked if there was a Mr. Clements in the room. I was totally shocked, not sure if he had said my name, and did not respond. He waited a few more moments and asked again, "Mr. Clements, are you here?" I slowly raised my hand, and he stared at me and waited a moment, then asked me to meet with him in his office after class. I was traumatized, wondering why he wanted to talk to me. At that time I had no interest in the thirteen colonies, the Declaration of Independence, the constitutional amendments, et cetera. I knew there were other students who had failed an exam or two.

After class I stood in front of his office door, and when he arrived, he opened his door without a word. He went in and sat at his desk and thumbed through his grade book. He verified I was Mr. Clements and went on to confirm that I had failed both of the exams and there was only one remaining test and a final exam in the class. He then spoke to let me know this was spelling trouble for me. He further sympathized with me and pointed out that not all people are college material and proposed that instead of wasting my time, I might consider transferring to a trade school. My heart began to throb after hearing I was not college material, and it began to echo in my mind. I looked at him in shock and felt devastated. My only reply was "OK, thanks for the advice." I did not know what else to say.

So I lowered my head and shoulders slowly walked out of his office and made my way to a bench in a secluded part of the campus where I thought about how I might tell my parents and friends that I had gotten kicked out of college. I sat there thinking how hard

Distraught, fighting accusation of "not college material"

my parents had worked to help me get into college and how they and all my friends were so proud of me. With tears welling in eyes, I made a decision and promise to myself. Since I had not actually been kicked out, I did not have to quit, and they would have to kick me out before I quit.

Maybe his words spurred me on to study harder because I did not drop the class, nor did I repeat it, but I don't remember what grade I finally got in that class.

Rejection by Fellow Engineering Students

After a year in college, in 1963, I dealt with another devastating racial incident during my coursework. I was taking a difficult thermodynamics class. It was a required class for engineers. I was hanging in there but struggling. I found out that there were several students, eight or ten, meeting before class in a room, reviewing and comparing notes on the assigned homework before turning it in. I walked into the room and began speaking to the students there—all White. I was able to solve most of the problems but was having trouble with a few of them. I walked over to one student and asked if he had made any progress on a particular problem. He looked at me and simply turned his back and walked away. I was surprised and my feelings were hurt, but I let it go. I then decided to approach another student and asked if he had made any progress on another problem. He rudely turned his back and walked away. At that point I got the message and accepted that that was the way it is going to be. I felt quite hurt, angry, rejected, and dejected. I decided to accept the fact that I was not going to get any other students to share information or work with me, and I would have to make it on my own. So that is exactly what I did. I think I got a C in that tough class with no help, all on my own. Other students failed the class.

Chemistry Class Surprise

I never took a chemistry class or anything close to it in high school. I could not relate to the subject. I did not frequent the library in high school. In fact, I don't even remember where it was and never knew its value. However, in 1963 there were specific requirements to complete a college-level chemistry class. I found myself in a beginning chemistry class during my second year. The class was held in a big auditorium, which was much less common during those days. There must have been nearly one hundred students in the class. The instructor was tough and had a reputation for failing half the class. There were four tests and a final exam. I studied hard to pass the tests while not necessarily becoming knowledgeable in the subject. On the first test, I received a score in the sixties. This corresponded to a grade of F.

We had three more exams to go. I again studied hard to pass the test, not focusing on understanding the material but rather on memorizing key points to pass the exam. Unfortunately, I was consistent in my test scores, receiving a slightly lower score and another F on each of the following tests. I was doomed since my only chance at being saved was to crush the final exam so that I did not have to repeat the class.

At last the final exam date arrived. I went to the auditorium early at 10:55 a.m. with my slide ruler and notes to try to astonishingly crush the final. When I opened the door to the auditorium, it was completely empty. I was confused and began to panic. Was it supposed to be held in another location? Did I have the right date? Also, seriously, I thought I might be losing my mind. All the final exams for all classes at the college were listed in a booklet that was given to all students. I grabbed a booklet to check the schedule. The location was right. The date was right. The scheduled time was 8:00 a.m. to 10:00 a.m. I looked at my watch; it was 10:55 a.m. I had been sure the exam was from 11:00 a.m. to 1:00 p.m. I felt screwed! I did not know what to do. Eventually I mustered up enough courage to go to the professor's office and tell him I missed the exam. My gesture was to simply be courteous so he could keep his records straight.

I arrived at his office several hours later, and he was there. I explained the situation to him. He said, "Let me look at my records." I really did not want to be embarrassed by him looking at my performance. He shook his head and said that I had been doing terribly in the class. I thought he was going to ask why I even bothered coming to his office. He said, "This is what we are going to do: return in five days to my office to take the final. This will give you time to study." I was not particularly grateful since I knew it was hopeless. However, I agreed.

I studied the best I could and returned to his office at the agreed-upon time and date. I took the final exam, which was as difficult as I had expected. I turned it over to him, along with the common postcard the professors used to mail the grade since the process to post took so long. I went home to my parents' house and waited a few days for the grades to start arriving. I wanted to intercept the F grade in chemistry before my parents saw it so I could explain what had happened. Finally a postcard arrived from the chemistry class. I was not excited because I knew what it was going to show. When I looked at the grade and saw a D as the final grade, I thought I was seeing things and wiped my eyes. If it was correct, I would not have to repeat the class. I let out a scream that could be heard throughout San Pedro. That was the happiest grade I have ever received in my entire life, even to this day.

Stellar Track Career

Beginning in 1962 I continued to set school records in the 440-yard dash at freshmen and varsity competitions at CSULB. I was the anchor on our four-man mile relay team. We were invited to participate in several local televised events, including the Los Angeles Times Indoor Games and the Sunkist Invitational at the Los Angeles Memorial Sports Arena. The biggest event was the nationally televised

Coliseum Relays at the Los Angeles Memorial Coliseum. It was a great honor to run against the best teams in the nation, especially since we were a college and not a big-time university.

Unfortunately, the worst thing imaginable happened. I usually anchored our mile relay team, but this time I ran the third leg, as suggested by the coach, thinking that was the best strategy. Our second-leg runner was Kerry, who came around the turn in the lead. I saw him enter the

Jack and Walt on the track

exchange zone, but he was too burnt out, and I took off too soon. I had to turn around since he had not put the baton in my hand. We juggled and dropped it. I had to run back and pick it up, but it was too late. We lost the race, and sadly nobody said a word to us. We had our chance to show the nation our strength, but we blew it.

Nevertheless, our team continued to run together in other events, and we won several races and championships. My brother, Walt, also came into his own and started winning races in the 440 hurdles. We were featured in the local newspapers.

Olympics Hopes Shattered

One of the saddest days of my track and field career happened during what turned out to be my final track performance. I was having a great year. I broke Ron Alice's school record in the 440-yard dash (47.1 or 46.7 for the 400-meter). Ron later became the track coach at USC. I set several meet records and most importantly qualified for the Amateur Athletic Union (AAU) and the Olympics trials. At the track meet against USC, I decided to also run my second-best event, the 220-yard dash. I had already won the 440. I was quite cocky and self-confident during this era.

The starting gun went off, and I tore out like a bat out of hell because I thought I could break the school record for CSULB. About three-quarters through the race, as I was coming around the curve, it happened. I felt a painful jolt and snap in my right back thigh area. I immediately tried to slow and stop. I did not fall but stumbled to the side of the track and leaned against the wall holding my leg. As I stood there grimacing, I saw everyone staring at me as they groaned. I knew I had torn a hamstring muscle. Tears began flowing from my eyes. Everyone watching thought I was tearing up because of the pain. It did hurt, but I couldn't have cared less about the physical pain. I realized that my track career was over at that moment. There was not enough time to heal and recover from this pulled hamstring to compete in the Olympics trials happening in a few weeks. I continued to stand there leaning against the wall. I saw my coach, Jack Rose, sprinting over to me, but I could see he knew it was curtains for me and my Olympics ambitions. I sucked it up and never competed again.

Dad's Work Accident

Back home in San Pedro, Dad had accrued several years of service at the Columbia Steel Mill in Torrance. He had moved up to become a bucket operator and was responsible for inserting the large steel plates into the giant rollers. Apparently, he had gotten down to investigate something near the rollers and a misfortune occurred. His right leg got wedged and crushed under one of the rollers. They had to stop production at the plant and rush him to San Pedro Hospital. My mom was called. I was at school at CSULB when she finally contacted me and Walter. We managed to get home.

They kept him in the hospital, trying to save his leg. Unfortunately, they had to amputate his leg about two inches below the knee. After months of rehabilitation, they fitted him with an artificial leg. He learned how to walk and managed to deal with the handicap. He eventually walked so well many people did not realize he had an artificial leg. He did not want to consider himself handicapped. In fact, a few years later he would go onto the roof of our house to fix tiles. He managed to live long after that with no obvious handicap signs.

LACBPE and New Fraternity Chapter

In the midst of my engineering struggles at CSULB, I was fortunate to join and become a part of the Los Angeles Council of Black Professional Engineers (LACBPE). This was a small locally based engineering organization designed to support the local Black engineers. It consisted of about thirty engineers each supporting our engineering endeavors. It was very needed and eventually grew to a few hundred.

It helped spawn the nationally recognized National Society of Black Engineers (NSBE). I am a lifetime member of the LACBPE and will always cherish their timely support and guidance.

I eventually also made a legacy contribution at CSULB with the creation of the Epsilon Kappa chapter of the Kappa Alpha Psi fraternity. Seven of us pledged and became members of the Kappa Alpha Psi

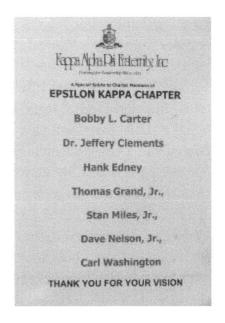

Kappa Alpha Psi Fraternity Inc

A Special Salute to Charter Members of
EPSILON KAPPA CHAPTER

Bobby L. Carter

Dr. Jeffery Clements

Hank Edney

Thomas Grand, Jr.,

Stan Miles, Jr.,

Dave Nelson, Jr.,

Carl Washington

THANK YOU FOR YOUR VISION

fraternity during our last year in college in 1967. The pledging process brought us all together as we bonded for life, having endured the grueling fraternity activities. We pledged in different chapters of the fraternity. Some of us pledged in the largest chapter located at the famed Los Angeles Kappa house of UCLA while others pledged under the Beta Omega chapter located at USC. We no longer felt isolated and became part of a much larger organization with national brotherhood activities.

During that time fraternity organizations were a very influential part of the community and the Black experience. The Frat Games, the Black and White Balls, and many other activities became popular throughout the community. The Frat Games consisted of rival basketball competitions between the four major Black fraternities. Bragging rights were very important. It turned out that some of the notable professional athletes of the future, like Wilt Chamberlain, played in the Frat Games.

The frat formal balls were elite social functions held by each of the frats, displaying elegance and sophistication with formal attire, formal dinners, and award recognition for community achievements. Often local dignitaries attended. In fact, the mayor of Los Angeles, Tom Bradley, attended the balls; prior to becoming mayor, he had been national president of the Kappa Alpha Psi fraternity.

The seven of us from CSULB were active in many of the fraternal functions and thought about forming our own chapter at CSULB. Our assertive leader, Dave Nelson, initiated the process. After about a year of planning, we formed the chapter and started our first pledge class. Recently I was gratified to find out that the chapter we created has gone on to become the largest, most active, and most productive of the Kappa chapters in Southern California. We had thirty members to start our first pledge class. It was fun and rewarding ordering those neophytes around to carry out all kinds of tasks for us. Despite some of the shocking hardships, those frat activities made some of my best days at CSULB.

The First

After my five-and-a-half-year, grueling education at CSULB, in 1967 I graduated and attended the graduation ceremony in upper campus. Afterward, alone, I headed down the hill to my car. As I was walking past the engineering building, I saw an elderly Chinese man approaching me. It was the dean of engineering, Dr. King. I had never met or talked to him before, so I assumed he did not know who I was. He walked up to me and said, "You're the first." Initially, I did not know what he meant. He then told me that I was the first Negro to graduate in mechanical engineering from CSULB. I did not know what to say, so I just stared at him for a moment. He congratulated me. I finally responded cluelessly, "Thank you. That's really good." He then slowly walked away.

At that moment I did not fully appreciate or recognize the accomplishment. I knew there was one other Black student in electrical engineering but no others in mechanical engineering like me. I went on home and told my parents and friends. I grew to appreciate the accomplishment more and more over the years. There were several recognition events that occurred later. The new engineering dean and a student leader from the NSBE invited me back a few years ago to speak at one of their annual functions. I was honored!

Chapter 8

Seeking a Mate

Marriage

Back around 1960 the cannery on Terminal Island in San Pedro was home to the tuna canning industry. This was a place where unskilled San Pedro residents could get part-time jobs during the summer break from college and other places. I had several labor jobs there removing large frozen tuna fish from boats and placing them on large wire racks where they could be rolled into ovens for cooking. The docks were slippery from all the fish, but I remember trying to pick up one of the very heavy tunas and noting the razor-sharp frozen fin on top of the tuna. If I were to slip and fall on the fin, it would no doubt slice my body and kill me. I was not injured during this period in my life because I was slow and careful.

During breaks at the cannery, my buddies and I would take a walk along the pier and look at the women standing outside also taking a break. As we walked by them, I noticed this one young, beautifully shaped young lady with a yellow, flowing dress. I looked at her, and she stared back at me. I went about my job but later inquired who she was. I found out she was the sister of Mattie, my classmate. Mattie and I were both in a class of 162 people who graduated from

San Pedro High School in the summer of 1962. I was able to get her sister's phone number and contacted Darlene later. We both worked there, and after we crossed paths a few times, I asked her out. We began dating, and I got a chance to meet her parents. She despised her father, partly because of his shallow education.

I was working on my Bachelor of Science degree in Mechanical Engineering (BSME) at the time. We continued dating, and in June 1968, we got married in the glass chapel in San Pedro.

This was soon after I received my BSME. My mother was never a big fan of our marriage, believing Darlene's family had completely different values than ours. Soon after receiving my BSME, I began working on my MSME while working full time in Costa Mesa, California, at Atlantic Research Corporation (ARC). This took a lot of time from our marriage and significantly contributed to our breakup.

Darlene and Jeff at their wedding

As time went on, we grew apart because of our family values, her relationship with her parents, and her treatment of my friends. She did not value a higher education nearly as much as I did and was mildly focused on getting a certificate in cosmetics. Unfortunately, her mother had convinced her that if she ever had a child, it would be deformed and hideous. I thought Darlene was exaggerating, but she believed this. This plagued our seven-year marriage. We never got over this since I really wanted to eventually have a family of my own.

Amiable Marriage Departure

We continued to grow apart, and after seven years of marriage, in June 1975, I drafted the divorce papers with her full cooperation. Darlene and I eventually agreed we were not compatible and needed to get a divorce. We agreed to split all our assets equally. I gave her most of the money in our accounts, and I kept our $27,000 house in Gardena, which had a $22,000 mortgage. I processed all the paperwork with no disputes or contests for a mere fifty dollars. There were no harsh feelings. We mutually went our separate ways and eventually lost contact with each other. I have only seen Darlene twice since then and would really like to know how she is doing. I hope she is living her best life.

Chapter 9

Through the Eyes of White Guys

The Mustache and the Nose Ring

After I received my BSME from CSULB in 1967, my first job interview took place. I went for my interview well dressed and groomed, and I had a neat mustache to make me look a little older, I thought. Anyway, I had ten interviews and no offers. The coordinator called me into his office and asked if I had any idea why I had not received any offers. I had no idea. I did not think about any racial reasons since during that time there was a desire to hire Blacks and minorities. He suggested it may be because of my mustache. He further counseled that some customs are not really endorsed in the industry and recommended I might think about cutting it off for now. I went home to my Long Beach apartment and discussed it with my roommates. We all agreed I should do away with the mustache. So I did. Back at CSULB, after a few more interviews, I started receiving offers. It turns out I received one of the highest offers made. It was from (Atlantic Research Corporation) ARC for $750 per month. I was ecstatic—I was rich!

After I had been working at ARC for several weeks, something occurred that changed my life. One day I was sitting at my drafting table, and a big, six-foot-five, middle-aged White man (Bob) walked in front of my desk and stood there. Bob looked extremely enraged for some reason and had a frightening and alarming expression on his face. There were about thirty designers in this open area, all with drafting tables. Bob put his hands on his hips, and with the biggest, loudest, booming voice, while staring directly at me, he spewed out, "Why don't you put a ring in your nose and go back to Africa!"

I was completely stunned, especially since I hardly knew the guy. I did not know whether to be mad, retort, insult him back, or what. But something amazing happened. Three of the thirty or so White designers sitting in the back, who were more stunned than I was, got up, and sprinted to the supervisor's office. And within minutes the supervisor appeared with a security guard, and they fired him right on the spot and escorted him out of the plant. Several of the other designers gathered around my desk to comfort me and explain that not everyone thought or acted like that. They convinced me that that guy had a problem and that others there really liked me. That made me more cognizant of generalizing about people and races.

This event shaped my career and interactions with company personnel. I worked for Thompson Ramos Wooldridge (TRW) in Redondo Beach, California, Mechanics Research Incorporated (MRI) in Los Angeles, and finally ended at Hughes, which was eventually bought out by Raytheon in El Segundo.

Master's Dissertation Rejected

During the early 1970s, I was on top of the world, having received my BSME degree and making lots of money in my aerospace career, working near home at the Thompson Ramos Wooldridge (TRW) aerospace company in Redondo Beach. I was now confident enough to think that maybe I could earn a master's degree in mechanical engineering despite my dismal undergraduate grades. I casually applied for entrance, not realizing I was not really qualified to apply because of my very low undergraduate grade point average. To my surprise, I was accepted into the graduate program at the CSULB engineering program. I continued to work full time, went to school at night, and took a moderate load of classes.

A fascinating phenomenon occurred when I took many of the theoretical engineering principles and began to gain an understanding of their application to real-world problems. I began to apply this to my classes, and this caused my grad school grades to soar. I finished my graduate-level classes with just under an A average. The only remaining thing I needed to do was turn in my master's thesis, which my adviser, Dr. Bruce Torby, was very proud of. It was entitled "Dynamic of the Bifilar Pendulum." I got it typed by one of the top secretaries at TRW as they allowed both of us time to work on formatting the many equations in the thesis. My adviser had signed off on the work, and all the bells and whistles had been completed. The last step was to simply turn it in to the clerk at the library. We were so proud of this day.

I stood in the single-file line of about ten graduate students all waiting to give the official copy to the clerk. When my turn came, I gave my copy to the clerk with all the completed submissions paperwork, and she quickly thumbed through my thesis. She then took the document, handed it back to me, and said it was *not* acceptable. Initially I did not know what to say. I just stood there to see if she was serious. She asked me to stand aside so the students behind me could be processed. I did not budge and asked why she had said it was not acceptable. She said the font was not an acceptable font. It turns out the school had an archaic sheet that listed all the allowable fonts. Could this obsolete sheet be used to reject my intense six-month effort, working with the top secretary in a premiere company that had just used the same font to win a multimillion-dollar proposal?

I said OK to myself and decided to go back to my adviser and ask for his help. He said no problem and that he would work it out. After several days passed, I decided to ask him about the status. He said he was having a little trouble getting it past the administrative people. I knew I had been working on this thesis for two years and my new position at TRW was contingent on me obtaining the degree and the degree was contingent on the successful completion of the thesis. I panicked and wanted to hurt somebody. I waited several more days as my professor struggled with the bureaucracy, even though the engineering department was behind me and the whole issue was ridiculous. I decided to contact the head of the college administration myself and explain the absurdity of the whole issue. I did, and he said he would get back to me. I waited several more weeks and became extremely desperate as it seemed my whole life might unravel. I and many others had made too many sacrifices to let everything slip down the drain because of a font.

I really pushed the issue and somehow made an appointment with the dean of the college in his office. I remember my mind was spinning as I was so desperate and mentally unstable with so much anger and intense frustration and was about to become unglued. I had the backing of the entire engineering department as well as my work colleagues. On the confrontation day, I walked to the dean's office with my latching, rectangular, vinyl briefcase with only two things in it. When I got inside his office, I was a complete mental wreck. Not able to speak, intensely wound tight with as much anger and determination as one could possibly imagine, I sat down, and he addressed me by claiming, "You are the person who has been raising so much trouble about this thesis font." I replied affirmatively. He admonished me about how rules had to be followed at that college and asked to see my copy of the thesis. I unsnapped my briefcase, not allowing him to see the two objects I had in it. I handed him the original thesis. He looked at it and further lectured me on following rules. I continued to tightly control myself so as not to become hysterical. He could probably see the intensity in my eyes and in my demeanor. He finally acquiesced, making a one-time exception, and admonished me to never pull such a stunt again. I said OK. He handed the thesis back to me, and I put it back into my briefcase, keeping the other item concealed, and closed the latch. I said thank you and walked out thinking how lucky *he* was.

Unforgettable Presentation at Church

I was a relatively quiet and shy person most of my early life, especially in front of groups or audiences. This all changed on May 21, 1975. I had finally received my master's degree from CSULB. I was very proud of that accomplishment, but my parents were "over-the-hill" proud. In fact, they had invited me to come to the church and say thanks to some of the members for their prayers and support and say a few words. I was quite reluctant to make this appearance, but they would have been very disappointed if I had not obliged. I agreed and braced myself to expect about twenty church members who I knew and had chatted with over the years.

My comments were scheduled for late Sunday afternoon. I headed over to the church, and when I arrived, I saw very few cars on the street or in the small parking lot. I went inside, and no one was there. I was completely puzzled. Did I have the wrong date or time? I went into the back and saw one of the custodial members, who directed me to another church up the street. I knew the place he was describing. I got in my VW and drove to the other church. I was slightly late because of my confusion. I entered through the side door. I peeked inside and could not believe what I saw: a packed church of well over a hundred people. I started to back away but saw my mom at the front table frantically calling me to come in.

I went in and headed into the audience to find a seat. She started waving again for me to come up to join them at the dais, where about ten people were already sitting. I reluctantly went to the front table, dressed in my casual clothes, and joined all the others dressed in suits and ties, along with the minister. At this point I was terrified and wanted to run away. My mom pointed out I was late. They had already said the opening prayer and were serving food. I remember having some green peas on my plate. I could not swallow a single pea because my throat was so dry from fear. They had a nice, simple printed program, and everyone had copies in their hands. I took a glance at the program to see what was planned. I just about fell out of my chair when I saw "Keynote Speaker: Jeff Clements." I was in total disbelief. I was very disturbed by my parents putting me in this predicament.

I looked to my side and noticed the side door of the sanctuary was still slightly open. For a few seconds, I contemplated bolting out the door. The repercussions of that seemed even more ominous, so I stayed and tried to eat the green peas. I had written some rough notes related to what I wanted to talk about in my presentation. My turn finally came, and I was introduced. I walked up to the podium and looked out at more than a hundred people staring at me. I was so nervous my eyes became blurry, and I could not focus on any words in my notes. *What should I say?* I thought about revealing how the most dedicated parishioners always sat toward the front and the others sat in the back. So I began talking about that. I continued to talk for about fifteen minutes, and I finished. I said thank you, and guess what? Everyone in the church gave me a standing ovation. I could not believe it; I had no idea what I had just said. After that traumatizing event, speaking in front of people or audiences has never been a problem for me. If I overcame that ordeal, I could speak anywhere. In fact, I now relish the opportunity to do so.

Chapter 10

Securing a Binding Family

Dating and Searching

In late 1976 I went to many social functions to meet people, especially pretty women, with the thought of marriage and starting a family. There were lots of nightclubs (e.g., Mavericks' Flats, Checkmate Club, the Parisian Room, California Club) and house parties if you were in the "in crowd." My buddies would scour Los Angeles and quickly figure out the whereabouts of weekend party action. We had no cell phones or pagers, just word of mouth. I met lots of ladies and collected a bunch of phone numbers; I followed up on some. Some of the numbers were phonies. I ended up meeting and seeing several young ladies.

During this period I was working on a major project and undertaking. It was called Automated Health Testing. There were a few books then on the concept of a customer walking into a medical clinic and having an enormous number of noninvasive tests conducted. The meaning of some of the test results may not have been immediately known, but the specific data was recorded to be used later. It was an epiphany that I fell in love with. With this notion I began to identify and amass a collection of all kinds of tests and test equipment. We called the project the Health Evaluation Center (HEC), and I formed a team of businesspeople, engineers, nurses, technicians, and several others in developing it. At the peak of the project, there were at least forty people involved.

The word got out that a major project was being embarked upon. A friend of mine, Tracy Rogers, knew a medical student Eugenia (Jean) Davis whom I should consider joining the project. He arranged for us to meet at his apartment in Marina del Rey. My friend Herman and I were at Tracy's apartment first. Soon Eugenia walked through the door. My mouth probably wanted to fly open as this gorgeous, voluptuous woman walked through the door. We chatted for a while, and I was blown away by how much we had in common in terms of the things that we enjoyed. She was in her third year of medical school. I was totally mesmerized and awestruck. I asked for her phone number so I could tell her more about the project and how she could help. She gave me her number. That night I called all ten of the beautiful girls I was seeing and announced I had found the girl of my dreams and may not be contacting them for dates but that we could remain friends.

Jean

Jean was a superstar by all the measures that were important to me. She was very attractive, with a shapely body, beautiful eyes, a lovely smile, and long, curly, mahogany-colored hair. She was a very honest and open person, and we really enjoyed talking to each other. She could play the piano and the viola. She was very knowledgeable about classical art and classical music, knowing the names and something about the artists of a lot of the works. These were all qualities that I did not have, nor had I ever thought much about such things. She opened my mind to new ideas, and these ideas sparked my interest. She was from a well-respected family in Atlanta, Georgia, and had a sister who was well on her way to excelling in the State Department as consul general, president of the Foreign Service Institute, and ambassador, reaching the highest rank achievable by a foreign service officer.

After we met, we succeeded in accomplishing an unbelievable feat. It turns out that we were together every single day for over 365 days, which we call Austin days. Austin is my middle name. We didn't plan to do that. It just happened—365 days. We did everything together; I introduced her to my parents on Christmas Day and to all my friends during this time. She was in school full time at UCLA School of Medicine working on her MD degree. She inspired me to later apply to the PhD program at UCLA. Prior to that I had had no intention of spending any more time studying engineering in school. But since she was there, we could both be there working and going to school. So I applied to the UCLA PhD program in engineering and got accepted.

Cooking or maintaining a tidy room were not her strengths. Jean was a worldly person with a breadth of global knowledge that was astonishing. I enjoyed every minute with her, and we did everything together. The one difference between our personalities was UCLA had given her so many headaches and challenges that her self-confidence was shaken. This was so different from her time in high school and even college when she was very self-confident. On the other hand, during my time at San Pedro High School and CSULB, I received very little support from the school counselors or staff and had to learn to manage just about everything on my own. This made me extremely tough and independent. To this day I don't expect much help, and I don't depend on other people. Jean tended to depend on me for many things, including entertainment, social activities, and business decisions. She pretty much let me be the boss when it came to business-related issues. And we hardly ever argued. This relationship worked for us.

HEC Project

In 1974 as mentioned above I embarked upon the most ambitious project of my life. It evolved after I developed a strong interest in the medical field, specifically biomedical engineering. I believed that personal noninvasive data that could be useful as a baseline or comparative information for evaluating personal medical information of all types should be collected from all individuals. This data would

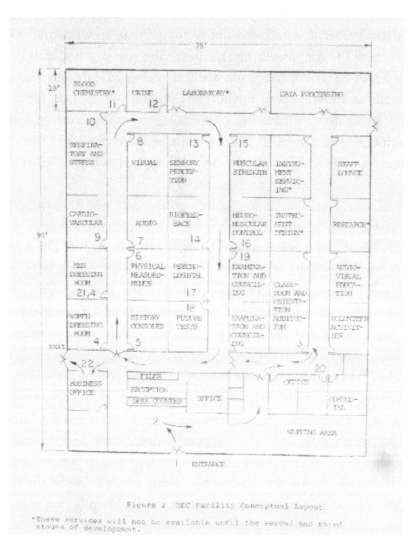

Figure 2　HEC Facility Conceptual Layout

*These services will not be available until the second and third stages of development.

include heart rate, urinalysis, respiratory functions, hearing, taste, reaction times, balance and strength, EKGs readings, tactile sensitivity, hair analysis, cognitive evaluation, visual acuity, and much more. This information would be organized and stored for current and future use. There was recognition that many diseases and ailments could be prevented or minimized with early detection. In times past, scientists had similar ideas and had documented them in books under the concept of AMHT (automated multiphasic health testing). I did a lot of research and found out there was no clinic or facility in existence that performed services like these.

I initially focused on what type of noninvasive health test could be conducted. I searched for all types of instrumentation and measurements of various health parameters. It was very fascinating to me, and I captured many brochures and much information. I started documenting some of my thoughts and amassed a listing of all the equipment and corresponding measurements that could be used. This was a major concern in the medical community. I started putting together a plan that involved creating some type of clinic that would measure indices and present them to the patron and allow them to have a record of all the findings. I talked to others in the medical and biomedical fields about this idea, and they thought it was an excellent idea to pursue. We believed we could collect and store the personalized medical information using technicians without engaging the services of highly trained and expensive medical doctors. We would engage the physician at the appropriate time.

I got extremely involved with the planning and creation of a clinic and solicited the expertise of different people. Everyone I talk with supported the approach and wanted to be a part of it, including my future wife, Eugenia. I decided to have a few meetings with key people to see if the idea of a health evaluation center could be made into a reality. We initiated some extensive planning, including facilities, equipment, people, budgets, costs, operational logistics, and so on, and it all seemed to be coming together. We documented the plan and managed to meet with the director of Harbor General Hospital and some of his staff. He was supportive and said that nothing like this existed and would be welcomed. He suggested that we needed to get the unions to buy in as they might be a steady resource for patients and clients to patronize the clinic. The project was moving along so well that it was clear we needed an office, secretarial help, and fundraising plans. I rented an office on Hollywood Boulevard that had a secretary and conference room that could be shared. I then started working on the project full time.

We needed to raise money to purchase the medical equipment and other expenses so we needed to find out how we could raise the capital. To seek help, we arranged to meet with Berry Gordy's brother, who had an office nearby. We presented the project to him, and he said he would help once we moved further along. It turned out that the people supporting the project included several doctors, lawyers, nurses, engineers, and other professionals. At our peak more than forty people were actively involved with the project.

Every aspect was moving along very well until we ran into a roadblock that was a game changer. One of the main features of the clinic was that we could use medical technicians, which would make the cost affordable. Someone put us in touch with the American Medical Association (AMA) and pointed out that if a physician was not associated with this clinic, it would not be acceptable. The AMA indicated that there were restrictions on giving out medical information directly to a patient without having a physician in the loop to review and approve the information. This went directly against the premise of the project of keeping the costs to a minimum and using less highly trained people to simply give the test and eliminate the need to have a high-powered physician in the loop. It turned out that we could not get around this constraint. We put the project on hold and were never able to resolve the problem.

The preventive tests were seriously damaged and constrained by these standards. We tried all the avenues we could to get around this problem, but we understood the medical profession's concern that giving medical data directly to patients might lead to inappropriate and unmanaged behavior. However, the cost of medical care was skyrocketing partly because of expensive labor costs and not taking advantage of less expensive labor when appropriate.

I finally abandoned my office in Hollywood and packed up at midnight to drive home. I'll always remember that while I was driving home, the song "Midnight Train to Georgia" by Gladys Knight was playing on the radio; it so much mimicked my retreat. I documented as best I could the things we had done and placed the information in a large notebook in case something came up or someone was interested in pursuing the HEC project in the future.

Unfortunately, the demise of the two-year HEC project did irreparable damage to my self-confidence and likely also to that of several others. I did not embark on any type of major entrepreneurship project at this scale ever again.

Life-Threatening Knife Fight

I had not traveled outside the United States before 1976. I only traveled out of state with my parents to Millington, Tennessee, to see my cousins and my grandmother. When I was on the CSULB track team, we traveled to a few places, including Fresno, California, and Oregon, to compete. I was not really interested in traveling out of the country until I met my fiancée, Eugenia. Her family lived in Atlanta. She had studied art in the Netherlands with Syracuse University during her junior year at Spelman, and her sister Ruth was in the foreign service. Ruth's career would eventually take her to many different continents and countries, including Africa, Italy, Spain, and Japan.

In 1977 we decided to visit Ruth while she was in Naples, Italy. This turned out to be a life-changing experience accompanied by some harrowing occurrences. Ruth had been promoted to consular officer from the United States. This would be my first trip to a foreign country. We were close to being officially engaged, and Jean wanted her sister to meet me. It was fun and challenging to plan our trip. We planned to take a plane, then a Eurail train from Mainz, Germany, to Naples, then to the consulate headquarters. We made it to Germany; Jean had taken two years of German in college but had forgotten most of it. We met a guy standing near us at the train terminal, and Jean asked in broken German, "Is this the train to Mainz?" They went back and forth trying to communicate, and he seemed to agree we were in the right place.

We boarded the Eurail train; there was a long walkway extending the entire length of the train on one side and several small booths adjacent to each other on the other side. We sat in one of the empty booths. It had room for about four to six people. We sat our bags on the seats next to us. Lo and behold, the same guy that Jean had just talked to came into our booth and joined us. He sat opposite us and directly across from Jean leaving only about six inches between their knees. He tried to make conversation with Jean, telling her she was doing well with speaking the German language. I just sat there listening and noticed he was a touchy-feely guy. He was constantly reaching to tap her knees. Since this was my first trip abroad, I thought these customs were aggressive and too friendly for me but perhaps OK there. Soon he started putting his hands on Jean's knees. She started saying, "No, no, no," and pushed his hands away. He persisted, and his efforts escalated. I had had enough. I grabbed one of our pieces of hand-carry luggage adjacent to him, lifted it up over my head, and slammed it down right next to him as it made a loud thud. I then waved my arms and yelled, "Stop it! Stop!" He jumped back and stopped. He got the message. He just continued to sit there motionless in his plaid coat. A few minutes later, he finally snuck a peak up with a sinister look. I am not a fighter, thug, or aggressive person, but something was not right. His seat positioning was blocking the door, so I could not easily move to get past him. He took his right hand and slowly slid it under his coat, still looking down with a sinister look. Something bad was about to happen. An awareness and feeling that I cannot explain overtook me. I lunged at him to grab his right hand. He resisted, and we both stood up. We wrestled for a moment as I had both of my hands on his right hand still under his coat. I saw he had something wrapped in a white handkerchief. The handkerchief finally fell off, and I was horrified to see a six-inch-long dagger. My adrenaline rushed up three octaves. We began to really struggle as I tried the get the blade from him. We struggled onto the long walking aisle, where passengers in other booths, as well as Jean, wondered why a Black guy (Jeff) was fighting a Turkish guy. The train stopped; I had confiscated the blade, and he ran away down the aisle alongside the train aisle. Jean was all shaken up and yet had not even seen the dagger. I thought to myself, *I have only been out of the United States in a foreign land for a few hours, and this is what has happened already.* Well, this story ended with the offender calling the police to retrieve his knife. They came, spoke little English, sided with us, requested the knife from me, and took the offender away because his ID paperwork was not current and complete.

That was the beginning of my first trip to Europe.

Ruth's Life with Bodyguards

When we finally arrived at the Naples train station, we were tagged by police as possibly transporting contraband, mainly because we were Black, but were released by the embarrassed policemen when the angry, Black, Italian-speaking U.S. consul got to the train station to retrieve us. We did not encounter any more traumatic events after that. In fact, the remainder of that trip was exciting and memorable, but Jean's sister was a little bit bossy, and I soon realized she had to be. She had a lot to coordinate, including her two ever-present bodyguards, the consulate affairs, and us. She would preplan our daily trips and suggest restaurants, museum tours, and travel arrangements. She tended to worry about us getting lost or in trouble, but I felt that was part of the travel exploration experience. During our stay with Ruth, we visited her friends, all very wealthy people with their estates, castles, and boats.

Ruth receiving military welcome in Africa

Several years later, we visited Ruth with our children when she served as consul general in Barcelona, Spain. Our last visit was with Ambassador Ruth A. Davis in the embassy quarters in Benin in West Africa, which encompassed about twenty-five thousand square feet. We stayed at the embassy quarters, which had three living rooms and two kitchens, servant staff, and security personnel. On one occasion she made arrangements for us to visit some of the slave castles on the west coast of Africa. It was absolutely heart-wrenching to see and hear the stories from the African tour guide of what happened there. I purchased a few books about the transatlantic slave trade and others about the local history of the events. It was so fascinating that I studied it for a few years and followed talks and documentaries presented in various venues over the years.

Gruesome Event

I struggled with whether I should include this highly gruesome vignette from when I was back in the States. I recommend that you skip this true story, which should be limited to only mature audiences as I would rate it X.

Jean and I were very close in 1976. We did a lot of things together and enjoyed each other's company. One evening we went to a club bar in Marina del Rey off Washington Boulevard. I'm not sure exactly how it started, but a guy, Martin, came over to us and pointed out what a great couple we seemed to be. He was White, about six-five, well groomed, and wore a curly, nice hairstyle and sported a large, dark mustache. We started a conversation, and he pointed out he wanted to meet somebody like Jean to be with. It turned out he was working on his PhD—I'm not sure where, but perhaps UCLA. I had already earned my master's degree in mechanical engineering and was contemplating enrolling in a PhD program at UCLA, while Jean was still in medical school.

He aggressively befriended me and Jean and wanted to socialize with us. We exchanged numbers, and he asked me to help him find a girlfriend. I told him both Jean and I would look among our friends for available candidates. It turns out there were a lot of nice-looking young ladies right there at the bar. Somehow we met this girl named Mary who was reasonably attractive; all three of us talked to her, and she felt comfortable enough to exchange phone numbers with Martin. He almost immediately fell in love with her, but he was a little awkward. He kept me up to date about his progress with

Mary, constantly striving to interact with her. I think she eventually became disillusioned with his constant desire to be with her, dominating all her time, focusing only on her. She started backing away from their relationship. He became obsessed with trying to maintain their relationship.

It turned out that she worked at the same company I worked, Systems Development Corporation (SDC in Santa Monica) in engineering but in a different location, and Martin asked me for a favor. Since she hadn't returned his phone calls, he wanted to know if she was still working there and asked me to visit the area, just to look and see if I could see her. I did and saw her sitting in an open area doing her business. I didn't introduce myself. I figured she would remember me. I went back and told Martin that I had seen her. I told him that it looked like she was trying to avoid him, and he should let it go and find somebody else.

He could not bring himself to let it go. We did not go out together anymore; I limited talking to him or interacting with him because he was too demanding and pushy. I was very close to Jean at that time. One evening, at my house in Gardena, I received a late-night phone call from the police inside Martin's apartment asking me whether I had received a call that evening. He asked me if I was Jeffery Clements. He asked me whether I knew Martin, and I said yes. He said he found my phone number in his book, and he wanted to talk to somebody about the situation. I said, "What's happening? What's going on?" He said Martin had done something that was not normal. I said, "What did he do?"

Martin had told the police that if he could not have Mary, he did not want anybody else. Then, apparently, he took his left hand and grabbed his penis and stretched it a little bit; he had a Coke bottle in his right hand. He broke the Coke bottle in his right hand, creating jagged edges, and proceeded to completely cut off his penis. I could not believe what the officer had just said. I had never in life heard anything like that. The officer said the ambulance was there, and they were taking him to the hospital. I said, "OK, thank you for letting me know."

I thought about it for a minute. I was in shock, and I convinced myself I was not going to tell Jean about this until much later. I truly felt fear about Martin's mental stability and sanity. I thought about it long and hard and concluded that if I were by myself, I might try to follow up and see what was happening with him. I was also unwavering that I did not want Jean to be involved with him anymore. That was the posture I took. I struggled with abandoning a friend, but this seemed like my only choice.

A few weeks later, I got a call from the hospital to give me some updated information. Martin was being cared for in the psychiatric ward. But I did not want to talk to him or visit him, and that's what plagues me to this day. I never heard anything else about Martin. I struggle with the question did I abandon a friend in need?

Chapter II
Raising a Family

Found Forever Mate

After our vacation in Europe we returned home a few years later. We got married on November 25, 1978, at Founders Church in Los Angeles, two days after Thanksgiving. We had a pretty good-sized wedding. However, there was one person who did not show up: Jean's father. He was a deeply religious man and a hard-core member of the Church of Christ. He believed my previous marriage to Darlene marred my marriage to Eugenia, causing it never to be legitimate or holy. He thus did not give Jean away at our wedding.

Eugenia and I were both successful in our careers. I worked in the aerospace field, and Eugenia became a physician, eventually opening her own medical clinic.

Kids Entered the World

Finally, after two years of marriage, the greatest news possible hit our home in Gardena—Eugenia was pregnant. We were ecstatic. Our entire village family was so happy for us and supported us in many ways. Malaika LaShan Clements was born on Valentine's Day 1981. Austin Louis Anderson Clements was born twenty-two months later. We had created our little girl and boy, and it was just like a fairy tale for me. We lived in Gardena in a nice three-bedroom, two-bathroom house. We enjoyed the community as the kids made lots of friends from the neighborhood.

The Two-Story Playhouse

Around 1986 I decided to build a fabulous playhouse. My wife Eugenia had always bragged about the playhouse her father built for her while she was a child living in Atlanta. Whenever any topic related to kids playing with dolls or in a dollhouse came up, she would bring out the fact that her father had built her a great playhouse. Well, I got tired of hearing the same story and decided I would do something about it. I would build a playhouse for my own two kids big enough for them to have fun in. In fact, it was going to be a two-story playhouse. I had no idea how to design and build a structure that someone could go inside, especially a little two-story house. Though I was a mechanical engineer and not an architect, I could still sketch something to get it built. I sketched something and showed it to the kids, and they were excited about the possibility of having a playhouse so they could invite their friends over and have fun inside. Austin was really excited about the playhouse and provided some great assistance throughout the project. I was so happy to see his interest level.

With the sketched plans, I determined what materials I would use to build it, including wood and beams. I designed a floor structure that would sit in our backyard and take up about a five-by-five-foot area right next to the back wall. So I started gathering materials from Home Depot, and I tried to include the kids in the venture. The floor was laid out using a plywood plank and wooden beams set directly on the ground about two inches off the dirt. I then made each wall using two-by-four beams as the kids watched me work, and they were so excited. I worked on the playhouse for several weeks when I had time, and it started to materialize into something they could believe would be their own playhouse. Little Austin was right there helping wherever he could.

A significant challenge was making a roof, which I hadn't thought about until I realized the house needed it. I decided to make a roof that could flip up and open for fresh air. So I left one side of the A-frame roof unattached. I had almost completed the two-story playhouse with an opening inside to get to the second level via a little ladder. As you can imagine, the kids started playing in the playhouse with their neighborhood friends before I had a chance to completely finish it. They were having a good time, and I thought it was reasonably safe. But that was not a good idea as one of the little girls, who was probably four or five years old, was on the second floor and didn't pay attention to the opening. She fell backward from the second floor all the way down to the bottom, landed on her head with a boom and scream. I was there and heard the thump and calamity that she caused. Tactfully, I examined the little girl, whose mother I had never met. While she was crying, I saw she had a couple of scratches and bruises, but she wanted to go back to play so I didn't make a big deal of it. I didn't want to reveal the incident to her parents or Eugenia. That worked out, and we kept our little construction accident to ourselves.

I finally finished and opened the playhouse for business with no major ceremony or grand opening. It was just a playhouse for my kids and their friends from the neighborhood. I had fixed it so that it was less likely that someone else would fall through. I have only one picture of the unpainted, unvarnished, and undecorated but finished playhouse. It did have a door, windows, and an adjustable roof.

Jeff built a two-story playhouse with kids looking from top

It was functionally the best thing for kids in the neighborhood. I don't recall Eugenia talking about the playhouse built by her father anymore.

One playhouse-related thing that did occur that I will never forget concerned our next-door neighbor. She was a White elderly lady who was about eighty or ninety years old. She lived by herself and seemed to be able to do all the work around her house. We were friendly to each other but only had minimal conversations. There were about five to ten neighborhood kids who played in the playhouse and who would sometimes gather around her house, and she would often give cookies to each of them. One day we were both outside watering our lawns but none of the kids were around. This bothered her, and she motioned over to me. "Sir, where are all the little pickaninnies?" she asked.

I was shocked to hear what I thought she had said. I said, "What did you say?"

She said, "Where are the pickaninnies?"

I realized she did not intend to be offensive. I was not sure how to reply to her, so I simply said, "I think they are back in school this week."

She said OK, and we ended our conversation. I never again had the opportunity to engage her.

Bigger House versus Free School

We planned, nurtured, and guided our kids through schools and various programs. One thing we took pride in was including the kids in nearly everything we did, even appropriate adult activities. On New Year's Eve, we would attend or have parties at our house or friends' houses in which all the kids were included.

As a learning experience, I made it a point to have them help write the checks for our bills. Malaika would fill in the correct amount from the bill, and I would sign the check. When we would go to the grocery store, I would get one shopping cart and let them have their own cart; I would let them go shopping separately, and we would meet and reconcile what made sense. I would point out what did not make sense to buy.

One big decision we made was to place Malaika at Frank D. Parent in Ladera Heights, a public elementary school that was ranked as one of the top schools, public or private, in Los Angeles. There would be no private school costs. This allowed us to shift the school money to buy a house in Ladera and not put money into a private school any longer. Malaika had spent two years in an expensive school for gifted children, but since we had two gifted kids, we made our decision. In 1988 we were able to buy a beautiful five-bedroom, five-bath house for $400,000, which took all the money we had saved for the down payment. This turned out to be a great decision.

Malaika whizzed through Parent School, receiving awards and recognition and making lifelong friends. Austin had enrolled in

Parent School, but the school had started to decline because out-side community people had started going to the school but did not adequately support or participate in the school's well-being. Austin did well in school but had a problem because of some of the teachers. One problem was the teacher felt his science project was not good enough, and after I, who had been a science fair judge, spoke with the teacher with my calm demeanor, his report was not turned in with his science project at the final judgment (purposely?). When we went to the fair, the judge told us he prob-ably could have won if they had turned in the report with the project. It was a lesson about jealousy for us all. Austin had won in the prior year.

Active with Kids' PTA

We became very active in the Parent Teacher Association (PTA). Mary Chitty was the president of the Parent PTA while James Chitty was the brilliant community organizer who put together tremendously successful fundraising functions. We also produced annual Halloween events that brought together the entire neigh-borhood, creating lasting relationships with the parents and kids of friends like the Townsends, Olivers, Williamses, Johnsons, and others.

Austin graduated from Parent School, and we bused him to Pacific Palisades High School. That school was not a good fit for Austin or us, so we enrolled him in a private school called West Los Angeles Baptist (WLAB) School as the high schools in our area were known to have gangs. Austin excelled at WLAB. He was quite popular, won the talent show he participated in, became student body president as a senior, and received stellar grades.

Motor Home to Disney World and EPCOT

When the kids were about six and seven years old in 1988 we decided to take an exciting and exploratory travel vacation. It turned out to be one of the nicest events we participated in as a family. The kids would have the opportunity to see other parts of the country, visit Disney World, and explore new experiences. We decided to rent a motor home and drive all around the southeastern portion of the United States. We planned to go to Florida, then up the coast, through Tennessee, west to Mississippi, and back south to New Orleans, forming a gigantic rectangular travel path. We planned on staying at various RV camping sites and stopping to visit and tour various attractions. Since none of us had experience with any type of trip like this, we had to do our research about motor homes and safety, as well as how to find places and then navigate to them. Since this was an adventure for all of us, we attempted to engage the kids as much as we could.

The big departure day came, and we flew to Florida and located the motor home rental company. However, our first big trauma was about to occur. When we got there, the motor home we had booked wasn't available, so we had to get a different type. I was very disappointed and was about to throw a fit. Then they told us the good news: the only one available was the largest size and new, and there was no added rental fee. I was initially excited but then thought, *I have no idea how to drive this dude.* No problem. A few minutes of lessons were available right away. The rental guy showed us both how to back it up about ten feet and how to go forward. Then he congratulated us and told us we were now certified to drive this motor home whenever and wherever we wanted. Eugenia and I were both still surprised that we were certified to drive this monster. We could now get on the road with this behemoth. We were both scared of the endeavor. I drove slowly. I easily made a right-hand turn onto the correct road, and we were on our way.

We followed the signs and pulled into the RV park in Disney World and easily found our slot. The various utilities included the water and the toilet hose hookup. We enjoyed ourselves in the motor home. It had a relatively large, nice kitchen, a bathroom, beds in the back for us, and beds in the front for the kids. The kitchen area had all the amenities of a home, and we used public transportation from there to get around in Orlando.

Our next adventure was to go to Disney World to see the Magic Kingdom and have fun on the rides, as well as see all the beauty and wonder of the place. We did all the usual things people do at theme parks on the first day and had lots of fun. We went to EPCOT Center on the second day. All our friends attested the kids would not enjoy EPCOT. Yet our kids were mesmerized by the exhibits, which allowed one to experience different parts of the world. They loved it.

We left the campground the next morning and headed north to our next destination.

One thing the kids really got a kick out of was, as we were going down the highway, we would sometimes see multiple-wheel big rigs alongside us. Somehow the kids knew how to get the truck driver's attention by moving their elbowed arm and side fist up and down. If a truck driver saw them, he would toot his loud horn, and the kids would both go crazy. Eugenia and I shared in the excitement and waved smiley thank yous back at the trucker. We, too, were proud members of the big-vehicles-on-the-road club.

We traveled to several states—up through Georgia, Tennessee, and down through Mississippi and Louisiana. We ate at some famous restaurants and spent time in the French Quarter. This was a real adventure and educational experience for the kids and us.

Honored at San Pedro Centennial Anniversary

In 1988, a big day came to the town of San Pedro. The centennial anniversary was about to take place. A committee worked hard to determine what and who would be in the special newspaper edition. San Pedro had been planning for this moment for several years. When the day arrived, there were all types of events, activities, shows, functions, publications, speeches, dinners, banquets, and so forth. One of the major components was creating a time capsule of some of the memorable events over the years, including a special publication of the San Pedro newspaper. For the capsule, they created a special edition focused on elected officials, the police department,  docks, and notable sports figures. They listed one hundred sports figures over the years with their pictures and names, and to my surprise, they included both me and my brother, Walt. This was the greatest honor we ever received, and we kept copies of the newspaper. I do not know exactly where they buried the capsule, but they had a big celebration for the burial, and it remains there. In the year 2088, one hundred years in the future, they will open it, and hopefully some of my progeny will be there to celebrate their ancestors, Jeffery Clements and his brother, Walt.

Chapter 12
Successes and Failures in Engineering

Aerospace Career Achievements

I had a stellar thirty-nine-year career from 1967 to 2006 in the aerospace industry. I designed and built spacecrafts. One of my early projects was the Viking Meteorological Boom Assembly. It successfully went to Mars and measured the planet's wind speeds and other atmospheric conditions. I later worked on the Apollo program, handling and assembling a part of one of the command module subsatellites (P&F subsatellite) that orbited around the moon on the first mission. It was the size of an office trash can and shaped like a tetrahedron. I also worked on the space shuttle, helping to evaluate the cargo bay and the spacecrafts that would fit inside of it. I worked on some key classified projects for space surveillance for the government and was on a tiger team to determine the cause of a failure on one of the company's orbiting spacecrafts that became inoperative. We had to figure out what the problem was and how to fix it. We formed a team of top-notch scientists and engineers and solved the problem.

Later I moved into management, where I headed an organization consisting of two hundred engineers and manufacturing personnel working together innovatively and synergistically. It was made up of both union and nonunion members. The facilities occupied several buildings consisting of assembly, specialty manufacturing, testing, and other labs. The lab organization provided much of the manufacturing for the company's space hardware and some of the tactical hardware.

My Frequent Promotions

I must brag that there was something about me that helped propel me in my aerospace career when I arrived at Hughes. Not exactly sure what it was, but it paid off. When I was hired at Hughes in 1985 by Ken Brown and Hamid Hague, I was finishing all the requirements for my PhD at UCLA. I merely needed to complete the publication of my dissertation. I came on board as a Member of the Technical Staff (MTS) and had no one working under me at that time. Within six months my boss came to me and told me I was promoted to group leader to supervise four engineers in my group handling both structural and gimbal design. This was a surprise to me, but I was grateful. I had never been a supervisor prior to this and was not that knowledgeable about the new gimbal design area.

About a year later, my boss came to me and told me I was being promoted to section head with two group leads under me. This again was a complete surprise, and I was grateful. My section worked on the design of certain components of a classified satellite system. The earlier version of the satellite was already in operation.

After another two years my boss, Ken, came into my office and told me I was being promoted to department manager and would supervise three section heads. I was shocked this time because that was the position of my then boss. My department would consist of about thirty engineers and scientists from such prestigious universities as Caltech and MIT. This was a real honor and challenge for me. He also pointed out that I could rearrange the organization as I saw fit. I studied and evaluated the organization and set up three new section heads and completed some other rearrangements. My rearrangements were appreciated and accepted. My department worked on some of the company's newest satellite systems and several research projects. I led that department for several years, then the new division manager talked to me one day about reorganizing and wanted me to run the entire space satellite manufacturing area. was a design engineer and not a manufacturing engineer. He told me that he knew I had the skills to get the job done.

I was promoted to assistant laboratory manager. This involved cable fabrication, circuit board manufacturing, and infrared (IR) radar systems manufacturing. All these added systems were new to me, but I was eager to take them on. I was later promoted to acting lab manager with just under two hundred people reporting to me. Many of the senior engineers were looking closely at the outstanding company-backed retirement plan, which was soon to end, and concluded it was foolish to continue working and not take advantage of the retirement package. So I took advantage of it and joined my retirement buddies. I am not certain why I was promoted so many times without asking for it, but I was always grateful, and I always got the job done.

Full disclosure: Ken is an African American. However, having me in his organization helped his career as he also received numerous promotions and became division manager, with over a thousand people in his organization. There may have been other promotions in the making for me, but I think I made the right decision for retirement as I planned to live happily thereafter.

Raytheon

O P T O - M E C H A N I C A L   D I V I S I O N

New Lab Emerges

(by Bernie Malis)

The Division welcomes the Engineering Development Transition Laboratory (EDTL) which has been formed by merging the D79 Product Operations Laboratory and the Prototype and Space Manufacturing Department. The new Lab is headed by **Dr. Jeffery Clements** while Pat Patterson, Manager, is on special assignment with the Raytheon transition efforts.

Dr. Jeffery Clements

"Our lab's new name reflects the fact that we are an organization in place to develop the processes, planning, and procurement strategies of developing engineering programs. Our success will be measured by the successful transition of these programs into other Raytheon manufacturing organizations for the production phases of the contracts," said Dr. Clements. EDTL's charter is to provide complete prototype and development manufacturing support for Strategic Space and Tactical Engineering programs. "The Lab will ensure that all hardware is manufactured to the highest quality level that our customers expect and require," he continued. "The merger of these two organizations brings together some of the best talent in the business. Its emphasis is on meeting schedules within cost, and providing assistance to engineering in all aspects of program engineering

development. We will continue to improve our planning, procurement, test, and delivery of engineering hardware through ongoing process evaluation and upgrades. Our team has substantial participation in IPTs, and all team members are committed to fulfilling their major roles in meeting the program goals."

Dr. Clements brings a full complement of professional and academic experience to his new position. He received his BSME and MSME from Cal State Long Beach, and continued on to UCLA where he earned a Certificate of Biomedical Engineering, an engineering degree, and a Ph.D. in Engineering in 1985. He held a series of technical project development positions with several companies before joining Hughes in 1984. Just prior to the move to EDTL, he held both project and line management positions in the Opto-Mechanical Lab. Dr. Clements has served on several Hughes panels and has been a member of the American Society of Mechanical Engineers (ASME), the Los Angeles Council of Black Professional Engineers (LACBPE), and the United States Tennis Association (USTA). A tennis enthusiast who occasionally plays tournament tennis, Jeff also enjoys meeting new people, and encourages employees to stop by and introduce themselves.

Major Aerospace Failure Nearly Took Me Out

I had lots of successes at Hughes but going back before my retirement one monumental failure almost took me down and out of the company prematurely. In 2004 my innocent actions threatened to shut down the entire Hughes facility in El Segundo. I was a department manager for the engineering sensor organization. I had about thirty engineers reporting to me, and in one of my sections, we were doing some advanced, state-of-the-art development in cryogenics. We were creating a cryogenic cooler capable of achieving 40 degrees Kelvin (-166 degrees Fahrenheit). This would be a breakthrough, with only a handful of companies and universities in the world striving for the same goal. Achieving this temperature would have tremendous applications in the aerospace world of missiles, in space telescopes, and in the medical instrumentation community. We were aggressively looking for additional experts in the field of cryogenics to come on board. Lo and behold, we ran across the resume of an individual, Rafi, with a PhD in cryogenics doing postgraduate work at UCLA. I got his resume and brought him in for an interview. Several of us interviewed him and were convinced he would be a marvelous addition to the team. I hired him, and he started working for Hughes. He was given company orientation literature to read and some general information about our department.

The following week I received a notice that the company attorneys wanted to meet with me. I was absolutely caught off guard and puzzled. I talked to my boss and a few others, and no one seemed to have a clue what it was all about. Reward or reprimand? The suspense was maddening. When I arrived in the main VP conference room, there were about five individuals waiting for me. They were all attorneys, including one corporate attorney who had flown in from out of state. They got right to the point and asked whether I was the one who had hired Rafi. I took a deep breath and answered yes. They inquired about which company literature Rafi had been exposed to. I thought for a moment and told them. They asked if I was familiar with International Traffic in Arms Regulations (ITAR). I indicated I had heard of them, but I was not completely familiar. ITAR makes up a U.S. regulatory regime to restrict and control the export of defense- and military-related technologies to safeguard U.S. national security and further U.S. foreign policy objectives. They then informed me that Rafi was a foreign national and not a citizen of the United States. I agreed with them that that made it very difficult to hire him. They pointed out that having a foreign national working in this highly classified facility for certain programs was a violation of the ITAR statute, and the government could shut down the entire facility. I stood there frozen and could not find words to respond. They then asked me to escort them to his location to retrieve all the documents he was exposed to. They would have security escort him out of the facility immediately thereafter. Sometimes as I sat at my desk over the next days, weeks, and months I thought about the ITAR issue. I never heard from Rafi or the lawyers again. My bosses said our human resources organization was supposed to catch these types of violations, but that was of little consolation to me. Nothing else ever came of it, as far as I know.

Selected to Be on Critical Tiger Team

While employed at Hughes, I was involved with the design and manufacturing of two classified earth surveillance satellites. One took three years to build, test, launch, and make operational. The other satellite was slated to be launched and become operational in a few months. The first satellite (a spy satellite) was very successful in providing a lot of valuable classified information to the government during a critical time for our national interest.

One day the company received a classified communication that the existing operational satellite had malfunctioned. They needed to figure out what exactly had happened and how to avoid it happening in future projects. There was further discussion of whether production of new satellite systems should be halted until the problem was fixed. To address this major problem, the company decided to put together a tiger team to investigate. Solving this problem was a very high priority for the company, and they pulled out all the plugs and made all the resources and personnel available to be extracted from other programs and assigned to this elite team. The tiger team would consist of experts in several different disciplines including optics, electronics, structures, and cryogenics. Some of the people needed were in or associated with my organization at that time. The team was to consist of about thirty people, who would have complete access to all the facilities, test equipment, and company resources. The company and the government highly valued this investigation both for its potential impact on the company's reputation and its bearing on any follow-up business with the government.

To my surprise, they wanted me to be on the tiger team. I did not have any unique specialty area, but I was knowledgeable in many of the areas considered critical for investigation. It took about a day for all the members to be gathered since many of them were already involved in other critical projects. The tiger team met in a classified building for a period of a few days. I was managing a large organization, but they wanted me to become dedicated full time to this tiger team. Anyway, it was one of the most enlightening experiences I have had in my career. We had the opening meeting. Steve, from the systems engineering organization, a very experienced and respected person, chaired the meeting. He recommended that we review all the relevant data and consider different ideas of what may have caused the problem and how to go about fixing it. He would consider everybody's ideas, no matter how far-fetched they might sound. Nobody was allowed to criticize any possibilities until each was fully examined to figure out if it could be enhanced. This approach was very interesting to me, and I could see how he was working it out.

For a few days we just brainstormed and reviewed data until we started homing in on the more likely existing problems. The probable cause appeared to be emanating from an electronic failure. A couple of the electronics guys started down a path that seemed to explain why the problem was occurring and what the cause might have been. They set out to do some quick experiments in the labs to see if they could reproduce the failure. Lo and behold, after a few days, they were able to simulate what they believed had occurred.

It was extremely complicated, but in layman's terms, the electronic boards have multiple types of electronic components soldered together in a precise manner. In outer space there is no air. It is a complete vacuum. The components with solder holding them in place can indeed behave slightly differently in outer space. Under certain circumstances, the solder actually can grow what they call tin whiskers. These little whiskers are smaller than a hair but grow out from the solder and can touch other parts of the electronic boards, causing short-circuiting. The scientists from electronics believed this was what happened. The industry was aware that this was a possibility but had not experienced it before. This was, indeed, a breakthrough in the industry. The information was shared among many other organizations and companies. They figured out a way to reroute the electronics and bypass the failed circuit board of the operational satellite, which corrected the problem. The tiger team was an exceptionally successful group of brilliant scientists and engineers that collectively solved a very complex problem. I felt honored to be part of the team. This was one of the most rewarding experiences I ever had that I will never forget.

Judge for California School Science Fair

Outside of Hughes, in 2001, while I still worked there, I was selected as one of four statewide judges for the annual Science Fair Student of the Year competition held at the California Museum of Science and Industry (now Caliornia Science Center). I was selected by the curator Dr. Ken Phillips. This statewide competition of junior high and high school students culminated with the selection of the Science Fair Student of the Year. This took several days of judging, which represented the culmination of the students' work over the entire school semester. The winner was a young female, which was rare in those days.

There was one other very rewarding interaction I had with young upward bound college students. I taught two college bound math classes for selected underserved students at Valley College. This was for advanced high school students who had qualified to go to college. The students were sharp, inquisitive, and almost certain to succeed in their chosen disciplines. It was very rewarding to be part of their development.

MESA Program a Big Success

One of the things I really wanted to do was introduce more minority students to opportunities in science and engineering. The chance came in working with Rhonda Hayes at Raytheon to bring a major Math and Engineering Science Academy (MESA) event to Hughes in conjunction with CSULB in 2004. The staff at CSULB had hosted the event over the years at their campus but never at a prestigious aerospace facility. The staff consisted of Dr. Tiggs, Ms. Saba, and many others from CSULB as well as several volunteers from Raytheon. Because of the secure nature of operations at Raytheon/Hughes, our request to have several hundred students enter the facility for the event was declined. The head of security did not say it aloud, but he was likely thinking, *No one would possibly allow six hundred wild minority kids to run around this tightly secured facility.* Rhonda and I did not give up and kept talking to the right people and managed to get approval to have the event only on the outside field of the facility itself. We had twenty-five or so events with teams of ten or more students from various schools competing. Hughes was extremely cooperative and allowed the students to get a feel for the aerospace environment. We were eventually not only allowed to have events on the open field outside, but the company cordoned off part of the inside facility and the students were allowed to compete in various events inside. The event was very successful and is one of the major highlights of my career.

Great Aerospace Accomplishment Not Recognized

One of my greatest accomplishments during my aerospace career was the creation of the Assembly Planning Readiness Review (APRR) in 2005. After the merger and reorganization of Raytheon with Hughes/GM, I was placed in charge of a portion of the engineering and manufacturing activities. One of the people I supervised was Maranda Williams, who oversaw the assembly planning section. Her staff wrote the detailed instructions for assembling hardware subsystems. This included identifying the specific hardware and correct part number, the parts to be cleaned, the order of installation, the type of fasteners to be used, how to tighten and torque the fasteners, and documentation of each step, as well as a periodic inspection schedule. Maranda's team had been doing this for years and was made up of very experienced planners.

One of the big problems they frequently faced was gathering the early attention of the engineers to get clarification of the engineering drawings and on occasion correcting problems with the drawings. These corrections caused serious delays, especially when they could have been caught sooner had the planners had access to the drawing at an earlier stage. Maranda and I discussed this and suggested we conduct earlier reviews with the planners and engineers. The engineers were very busy and claimed they did not have time to devote to this more structured review. My background was in engineering and drawing creations. Their objection made complete sense to me. However, I pushed back on this and picked one project as a test case to see how the engineers and planners worked together. Ron Townsend was the first project lead on this new endeavor. The review uncovered several major scheduling and rework problems. It also led to numerous corrections in the manufacturing planning process being made to the drawings, allowing the planners to begin working early. It was so successful that leaders of other projects wanted to conduct the APRR. I created and documented the process and format to conduct other APRRs. Soon these reviews spread to several projects and eventually to other programs involving many projects. The customer, the United States Air Force (USAF), was also very impressed with the APRR process and complimented the programs. I was asked to write a companywide procedure. I created the document, but I retired soon thereafter and never got to witness how widespread the APRR was adopted. I think industry adopted the process or something resembling it. I don't know. I was very proud of the APRR but never got credit for its creation. Nonetheless, over the years I made notable contributions to several aerospace programs including Apollo, Space Shuttle, Viking I, P&F Subsatellite, and Spy Satellites.

Nominated Black Engineer of the Year

It was with great pride that I accepted the nomination to be included in the exclusive list of national candidates for Black Engineer of

The 1991 Black Engineer of the Year

Television Special

January 2, 1991

Dr. Jeffery Clements
6170 Wooster Avenue
Los Angeles, CA 90056

Dear Dr. Clements:

I am pleased to inform you that you have been nominated for the Black Engineer of the Year Award. While the Selection Committee has not yet finalized its choices, receiving a nomination is a great honor, signifying that you are a distinguished leader in your field.

Because this year's awards program will be nationally televised, some of the winners will not be announced until that evening. In the next few weeks you will be receiving information about the award finalists.

Since you are a leader in technology, I'd like to invite you to be a part of the Awards Conference this year. Along with the exciting Awards Banquet with Ossie Davis as Master of Ceremonies, the conference will include an opening reception, student and professional career development seminars, a career and EEO job fair, a VIP reception, a cabaret concert, and a networking party.

With all these activities, the Black Engineer of the Year Awards Conference is America's #1 career-building weekend.

Again, congratulations on your nomination. Black engineers, scientists, and technology leaders are widening the frontiers of opportunity. I look forward to seeing you in Baltimore on February 28th through March 2nd for the fifth annual Black Engineer of the Year Awards Conference and Banquet.

Sincerely,

Tyrone D. Taborn
Publisher

P.S.   All nominees are offered a special discount on VIP awards banquet tickets. Fill out the enclosed registration form for up to 4 VIP tickets at half price!

TDT/mtb
Enclosure

CAREER COMMUNICATIONS GROUP INC.
729 EAST PRATT STREET, SUITE 504, BALTIMORE, MD 21202, 301-244-7101

the Year in 1991. My nomination emanated at the executive level of Hughes Aircraft Company from my boss, Mr. Ken Brown, championing the effort. The nomination process required much additional effort on my part to compile information about my background and many of my accomplishments as an engineer. They vetted my information via interviews with some of my previous employers, distinguished friends, co-workers, past and current, as well as professors and administrators from prior educational institutions. They believed they not only had a credible candidate in me, but my candidacy had a good possibility of winning. All this reflected honorably on Hughes Aircraft Company. The requirements to qualify as a nominee included my technical achievements, my management achievements, my community involvement, my education, and my real project completions. My application was nearly an inch thick. The winner announcement was made on national television. All the nominated candidates were very impressive, and the finalist was Guion Stewart Bluford Jr. (born November 22, 1942), an American aerospace engineer, retired USAF officer and fighter pilot, and former NASA astronaut. I was not disappointed, but happy and highly honored to be considered among such distinguished competitors. My company Hughes Aircraft was also proud, so much so that they later hosted a special banquet in my honor for achieving such a prestigious nomination.

Chapter 13

Epic World Journeys

Exploration of Countries and Continents

Around 2000 we went to Washington, DC, to see Jean's sister, Ambassador Ruth A. Davis, receive an award from the State Department. Ruth was, without exaggeration, one of the best public speakers of our times. Her powerful voice and delivery

President George W. Bush, Ambassador Ruth Davis,
and Secretary of State Colin Powell

would shake the room and keep everyone on the edge of their seats. She was frequently asked to speak as the keynote speaker at prestigious events. Ruth's 2001 speech in front of both President George W. Bush and Secretary of State Colin Powell was spectacular. President Bush said he never wanted to trail her again in giving a speech in the future and told her she reminded him of his mother, which she thought was nice but made her slightly uncomfortable.

We have been so blessed to have been able to visit so many parts of the world. Between Jean's diplomat sister, traveling with our close friends, and traveling on our own, we have toured many wonderful places in several countries on six of the seven continents.

Here are some of the places we have been fortunate enough to visit: the Great Wall of China, the Egyptian pyramids, the Sphinx, Machu Picchu in Peru, the Eiffel Tower, Tiananmen Square in China, Robben Island in South Africa, Maasai Mara in Kenya, the Louvre Museum in Paris, the Leaning Tower of Pisa, the Colosseum in Italy, the Galápagos Islands off Ecuador, and the Rod Laver Arena in Australia. Back in the United States, we finally made it to Niagara Falls

Jeff and Jean dining in front of the Egyptian Sphinx and Pyramid

in New York and Canada, Mount Rushmore in South Dakota, and Anchorage, Alaska, where I worked on the Trans-Alaska Pipeline. Given all the turmoil and unrest in many parts of the world, we are staying at home for the time being.

Lion Hunting

One of my greatest and most poorly thought-out adventures took place on the west coast of South Africa in 2005. A group of Los Angeles friends made a trip to southeast Africa to visit the homeland. During the trip we went on a safari to see wild animals; we were hoping to see some of the big five—lions, elephants, rhinoceroses, cheetahs, and leopards. We had ventured out most of the day and managed to see all of them except the lions and leopards. Being an avid watcher of nature shows on the Discovery Channel, I was generally the first to spot the hidden animals when we were on group tours. We had not seen any signs of lions all day. Our female tour guide said she would take us to a place where people had spotted a pride of lions a few days ago and perhaps we would have better luck there. The group had nicknamed me Scout because of my skills at being the first to spot wild animals.

Lions waiting for careless tourist to make a mistake

We made it to the top of a small hill with a great panoramic view of the surroundings. It was barren, with lots of three-foot-tall grass surrounding us. The guide said we could get out of the safari jeep but should stay near it. She and about four others got out on the left side, while my buddy James Bird and I got out on the right side. We had our expensive cameras ready to catch any movement of lions. I was intently looking for any motion. Amid the zeal of our search, we haphazardly crept toward the high grass, hoping to see something. The guide saw us venturing quite a way from the jeep and screamed out, "Get back over here close to the jeep! There might be lions lurking in that tall grass." We froze at her words and thought that if there were lions in that grass ten feet from us, we could be dinner. I was sure I could outrun James, but we both backed up slowly toward the jeep and got into it. We looked at each other and thought how reckless we had been. The rest of the group has never let us forget how daring and clueless we were and how they missed a good predatory scuffle. Later I got some hints that James may have had some hidden track sprinter skill.

Stranded in the Nairobi Airport

Talking with Maasai warrior

On the same 2005 trip, we were ready to end our magnificent travel through Nairobi, Kenya, having stayed in a village in the Maasai Mara National Reserve. All eight of our Los Angeles traveling companions led by James Chitty, had departed the previous day. Jean and I had a flight out at 7:15 a.m. the following day. We were slated to go to Cairo, Egypt, to see the pyramids. It was Sunday, and we got in a prearranged taxi with all our luggage early in the morning. It was dark. The driver headed toward the airport, which was about an hour away. He, like all the drivers in Nairobi, completely ignored the traffic lights. He flew through them like they did not exist. He did not speak any English, nor did anyone else in the service car. All the highway signs were written in a language we did not know, but we could kind of figure out what was going on. When we finally arrived at the airport, we managed to get to our airline to check-in. We showed the lady at the counter our tickets and passports. Fortunately, she spoke a little English. She looked closely at our tickets and had a puzzled look on her face. She said, "This plane has already departed. It left an hour ago." We looked at her in disbelief. I said that was not possible and showed her where the departure time was. She tried to explain some nonsensical reason why sometimes planes left early if full. We asked about the next plane to Egypt. We had already checked out of our room and began to panic. She said the next plane was leaving in the morning and it was already full; the waiting list, too, was at capacity. We panicked. We finally asked when the next available flight with seats that we could get on was departing. She said Wednesday at noon, and the current day was Sunday.

We ended up going to the problem office next door to plead our emergency. One lady pointed out we should come back early in the morning because the waiting list is recognized but "first come, first served" is what is actually followed. A fleeting thought crossed my mind that we might spend the rest of our lives in Nairobi selling fruit and ornamental trinkets. We did not think about contacting the U.S. Embassy.

We headed back to our hotel and managed to rebook the packed hotel for an unscheduled extra day. We went to the airport extremely early the next morning and luckily managed to get on the plane. Arriving in Cairo one day late, we had to cancel our trip down the Nile to Alexandria, but truly enjoyed our stay in Cairo. We made connections with a knowledgeable and friendly cab driver who offered to show us more in Cairo than we could have ever seen on our own. Highlights included: King Tut (who no longer travels in his sarcophagus outside of Egypt), the pyramids (with a big light show), and the Sphinx. The driver took us all around Cairo during the two days we had there. We had fun.

Egypt Camel Trade

We had a most remarkable experience with one of the Egyptian elites, and I will never forget it. We had made our way up to Egypt and into the great museum in Cairo. It housed some of the most famous ancient exhibits; Jean was able to stand next to the actual King Tut sarcophagus. We toured the amazing museum, inspecting all the antiquities and art that you could imagine. Some dated back thousands and thousands of years. We finally finished up and started leaving the museum and walked outside, where this nice Egyptian young man intercepted us. He pointed out how proud he was of the fascinating museum and asked if we had any questions. He said the Egyptian people in general were so proud of their museum. We chatted for a few minutes. He pointed out we should see something else, something only a few other people had seen. I think we were the only Blacks among about a hundred or so tourists in the courtyard. He seemed nice and trustworthy, and we asked him what he was talking about. He said his brother had his own business a few blocks away, and he wanted to show us something rare. We were hesitant, but he persuaded us to take a quick walk to see what he was talking about.

Jean standing next to King Tut in the Egyptian Museum in Cairo

We followed him away from the museum a few blocks. The journey involved a few twists and turns. We became concerned we were getting farther from the museum and seemed to be losing our sense of direction, and we kept wanting to turn around. He kept insisting that it was just around the corner. Finally, after what I would estimate to be about ten blocks, we arrived at his building. He said it was his brother's business. It was a very nice, beautifully structured building. So Jean and I walked inside, and he introduced us to his brother. He was about six-five and a well-groomed, handsome, firmly built man. We were amazed as we looked around the room and saw hundreds, maybe thousands, of cup-sized clear glass jars with decorative glass tops. We didn't know what they were. The owner pointed out that he had one of the largest collections of rare perfumes and scents in the world. There were shelves containing these little glass bottles all around the room, with about ten shelves on each wall. It was beautifully designed and laid out.

He pulled out some samples for us to smell as he proudly described them. We were indeed fascinated at the sheer volume of these scents. We asked a few questions, and he started telling us about the industry and how he had come to amass such a collection. He was very fascinated with Jean's appearance and her general attractiveness. He thought she was absolutely gorgeous. She had her hair tied up and resembled the Egyptian queen Nefertiti. He continued to rave about how beautiful she was. I said thank you several times and thought he was going overboard. In any case Jean had to go to the ladies' room and asked him if there was a restroom nearby. He said sure and described where it was, down the hall and to the right. So she left, and the three of us remained in the room. The owner pointed out to me that Jean was one of the most beautiful ladies he had ever seen; he said I was very lucky. He looked at me and moved closer, then spoke in a low voice, "I would like to make a deal with you. I'll give you one hundred fifty camels for her."

I was absolutely stunned. I had never heard anything like that, and I didn't know what to say. He was dead serious. I did not say a word as I was trying to comprehend what he had just said. He repeated, "Yes, one hundred fifty camels I'll give you for her." I still didn't know what to say. I started thinking about my options. Here we were in this remote location in which we knew nothing about our surroundings, the people, or whether we could navigate back to the museum. I didn't want to insult him, so I kindly said, "No, I don't think I want to make the trade."

He said, "I will throw in sixteen goats."

I was so stunned that I didn't know what to do. I could have run, but Jean was still there. I sat there for a few minutes, then said, "Well, let me think about it."

About five minutes had passed, and Jean emerged from the restroom and walked over to us. I knew my goal was to get out of there as soon as possible without breaking and running toward the door because she didn't know what was going on and I didn't want to explain it to her. So I said, "Let me think about it," and we started making our way toward the door. Fortunately, Jean did not express any interest in staying any longer and could sense that I was a little disturbed, so she followed my lead. We did not want to show alarm, so we casually walked to the door, giving him the impression that we might come back. His brother was kind enough to escort us back to the museum without any problems. So we left, and I did not tell Jean the story just then because she might've wanted to go back. I'm very proud to have such a beautiful wife who someone was so infatuated with that they would offer one hundred fifty camels and sixteen goats. Perhaps two hundred camels would have turned the trick!

Deadly Cancer Battle Begins

I need to go back a few years to discuss my awareness of cancer. During my employment at Hughes, in 1994, I was entitled to have an executive physical examination at the company's expense. During the exam the doctor did a digital examination and he felt a lump on my prostate. He suggested I get a PSA blood test. I did, and it showed I had a slightly raised level. We continued to monitor it for several months, and the increase started to become worrisome. We looked at the options of radiation treatment, surgery, or wait and see. With the PSA increasing relatively fast, we decided on surgery.

The surgery was done by Dr. Kaswick, the head of the urology department at Kaiser Hospital on Sunset Boulevard at that time. My daughter and his daughter were in the same grade at Mirman School for gifted children, which allowed us to have a good, candid doctor-patient relationship. He pointed out that if the cancer metastasized, I would only have about six months to live, based on experience with several patients in very similar situations. The test was conducted at Kaiser Hospital. The results would take about a week to come back. This was the most agonizing period of my entire life as I did not know if I had only six months to live. At home I started thinking about my life and my future. I decided to jot down my innermost personal thoughts for my wife, Jean, my daughter, Malaika, and my son, Austin. With tears streaming down my face, I typed my thoughts, sealed the document in an envelope, and titled it "Just in Case." This was 1994, and I have not looked inside since; it remains in my mail inbox untouched.

About a week later, a Kaiser oncology nurse called. She had the results. Casually she said the cancer had not metastasized. Unsympathetically she added, "That's all I have for now," and hung up. I was stunned at the abruptness of the call, especially since it was so critical for me.

Months later I had the surgery and began the lifelong recovery process of examinations, tests, blood chemistry processes, and various treatments. I became aware of the many men who had been in similar situations but were no longer around. Others completely recovered and have no lingering problems. The entire treatment process has significantly evolved and improved over the years. I am happy to be hanging in there to this day. I realize I am very blessed to have lived and experienced so many blessings in life, and I thank God for being my protector and best friend.

Mentoring Legacy

One thing that I am very satisfied by and proud of is my informal mentoring of incoming Black employees at Hughes, which lasted from around 1990 to my retirement in 2006. I hired one and worked very closely with three other young Black employees in their careers, helping them through the engineering obstacles at Hughes. We would talk informally when I was available to candidly advise them on their challenges. I really emphasized the need to be respectful but more assertive and to make sure they were not left out of important issues or meetings that might have a major impact on their progress. They all progressed exceptionally well in the company and received promotion after promotion. Even years after leaving Hughes, I still get calls and visits from them asking how I am doing and thanking me for the guidance I provided.

Chapter 14

Tough Family Choices

Son's Fork in the Road

Before graduating from junior high back in 1995, at which point we lived in Ladera Heights, Austin ran into a major bump in the road, likely from all the school switching turmoil or his hormones taking over. This led to one of the worst days of my life. Austin began hanging out late with some of his friends. He failed to let us know if he was coming home late. We asked him to just let us know if he was going to be out late, but he continued to fail to inform us. One night we were up past 3:00 a.m. and were struggling over whether to contact the police. Cell phones and pagers were not available yet. Finally he called and asked us to come pick him up in the Marina. I met him on a corner, and he gave no explanation. I was absolutely furious but was uncertain what I should say to him. He remained quiet. I could not believe the son I loved so much and nurtured his entire life had allowed this situation to transpire and had shown so much total disrespect.

On our way back home, I was so distraught that when we reached a fork in the road, I pondered whether I should continue west on the 91 Freeway or veer right to the ramp heading north. If we went north, I would drop him off downtown at the Los Angeles homeless mission. If I continued west, we would go straight back home to continue to try to correct the behavior. We went straight home, and Austin eventually became the most ambitious, productive, and wonderful son we could have ever imagined. Years later he explained to us what happened that night.

Kids' College Progress

One major factor behind Malaika's and Austin's success was attending Historically Black Colleges (HBCUs). Malaika enrolled at Spelman in 1998 and Austin at Morehouse in 2001. I learned that these colleges' big focus was to nurture and help the students through the whole experience. This was foreign to me because of my experiences in college. The kids formed strong, productive values and created a network of lifelong, successful friends.

After teaching fourth grade for about four years, Malaika went on to Loyola Law School and received her doctor of jurisprudence degree. After Morehouse, Austin worked in investment management for about four years before going to Stern School of Business at New York University (NYU) to acquire his master's degree in business administration. He met his wife, Crystal, in Los Angeles; she was from New York, which made life easier for him while he was in school there. He was able to stay in the apartment she was maintaining in Tribeca.

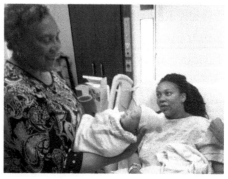

Both progressed extremely well in their careers and bestowed us with the greatest news: Malaika and

First grandchild to arrive (Ava)

her prized husband, Ken Billups, announced they were expecting our first grandchild, Ava. Austin and Crystal also lit up our lives at an informal family gathering, announcing in some tricky fashion that their first child, Chase, was on the way. Lastly, a few years later, Ivy was born to Malaika and Ken.

Daughter's Condo Burned

As I have mentioned, Malaika married her wonderful Florida A&M graduate and Kappa man Ken Billups III. They lived in a nice second-floor condo in a lovely complex just west of downtown Los Angeles, near Loyola Law School, and had given birth to a cute, little, grayish-blue-eyed daughter, Ava.

One evening in 2014, when Ava was less than two months old, Malaika and Ken smelled smoke. They checked but could not find a source, a fire, just smoke beginning to seep through the walls and light fixtures. As they searched for the source and the smoke became more intense, they called the fire department and evacuated their condo. The condo became consumed with smoke emanating from an electrical fire from the condo below. The fire damaged their bathroom, kitchen, ceiling, and roof. They had no place to go immediately, so we had them come home with us to our house in Ladera. Jean and I enjoyed their company and felt blessed to help rear Ava for just about the entire first year of her life.

Chapter 15

Unplanned Art Career

Wife's Guidance toward Art

After retiring from Raytheon, I had the grandiose idea of just kicking back, relaxing, and playing tennis in a few tournaments (see attachments 8 and 9). That all changed when my wife convinced me to go to the M. Hanks Gallery in Santa Monica with the organization she belonged to, The League of Allied Arts group in 2006. We went to the presentation, and I actually enjoyed it. Afterward, while I was meandering through the halls filled with all kinds of interesting Black art, it happened. I saw an interesting pencil drawing of an old, dilapidated farmhouse by artist Charles Austin. I thought to myself that this was something I could do, especially with my skills in perspective drawings experience from the aerospace industry. As I surveyed the artwork, I noticed the $20,000 price—this completely blew me away. I thought, if I could do my own rendition of this subject and charge only a tiny fraction, I would be delighted.

I went home, grabbed a large piece of paper, and began drawing. My rendition of the dilapidated farmhouse came out really good. A few days later, we took the drawing back to the museum. The curator looked at the drawing and was very impressed. He suggested if I created a few more drawings, I could have my own art show. My new career in art began. I did what he suggested, and the rest is history.

Art Shows and Exhibits

In 2007 I held my first art show, at my house in Ladera, and it was very successful. I created a website but only had a few customers. I believe two of the reasons for this were my prices and the fact that I had no reputation in the art world. My art now has been exhibited in a respectable number of art shows in a good number of cities. For me, setting up the booths was always hard work, as was efficiently packing each piece and the unassembled booth parts, literature, and business items into my SUV. It was quite fascinating to see longtime artists set up their tents and display art to make it impressive and attractive. I had a lot of customers come by and rave over my art, and I enjoyed talking to them. However, I did not sell much at that time.

I eventually had some great success when I set up my art show at the Frame Store in Culver City for three weeks. One day a worker from the store called telling me someone wanted to buy one of my paintings listed for $2,850. This was my highest-priced item. He wanted to know if I would accept $2,650. I was so excited that, showing no negotiating skills, I accepted the offer before he could finish his sentence.

Awards and Recognitions

In 2007 I was honored to be accepted to exhibit in several museums and galleries, as listed below. My biggest accomplishment came when I entered a juried art competition at the Barnsdall Arts Center. There were several thousand entrants from all over California. They accepted two thousand entrants to be judged over a few days of competition. They selected ninety winners, and two of my three entries were winners. I was delighted.

My works were also sold in the Art Auction 12 for the Long Beach Museum of Art, and they were featured in a three-month exclusive exhibit at the Museum of African American Art in Los Angeles. In 2016 my artwork was featured along with that of four other artists at the prominent Wilshire Ebell Theatre art gallery for a Black History Month celebration. In 2018, I was featured in the *Los Angeles Sentinel* newspaper for my engineering and art achievements. I was selected to be part of the 2019 Pan African Film & Arts Festival. The Macy's African Art Museum in Los Angeles featured my works in a three-month solo exhibition. As guest speaker at the 2019 NSBE Black History Recognition at CSULB, I was successful in auctioning one of my artworks for $2,500 for a student scholarship. I continue working on hosting art shows every now and then, but I also enjoy creating art at my own pace.

One of Jeff's art creation styles (dilapidated houses)

Chapter 16

Published Sci-Fi Novel

I had a powerful dream one night in 2007 and woke up amazed and able to vividly recall it. It was so moving to me that I thought I should jot down a few notes. As I began writing, it became more and more intense and more like a story. I got so infatuated with the story that hours passed, and I produced pages and pages of text. Over time I kept adding to the fascinating story and eventually created a manuscript. It became clear to me that this story should become a published novel. Having no knowledge of how to create and publish a novel at that point, I did an enormous amount of research and submitted an enormous number of inquiries. I learned how to create and tell a story. I created characters such as a protagonist and a villain, developed paragraph structure, found a professional editor and publisher, and so forth. Finally, in 2008, I published my first sci-fi

APHELION

Scientists fear a
mysterious
cosmic
phenomenon
threatens Earth

by
Dr. Jeffery Clements

novel, entitled *Aphelion*, on Amazon. I have hopes and dreams of it turning into a major movie production. Time will tell. Even though it did not make the bestseller list, I did have a few book signing gatherings, and it did pretty well.

Chapter 17

My Dad's Health Decline

My Dad's Terminal Illnesses

Over the years my father began to suffer from diabetes, which eventually required hospital care. The dialysis treatment left him feeling drained. Later he was diagnosed with prostate cancer. He elected to undergo radiation treatment and was never his old vibrant self after that. He lived for a few more years, never complaining to anyone about his medical problems. I distinctly remember on October 25, 2011, driving to San Pedro when a neighbor, Charlotte, called me on my cell phone to tell me to come to the nursing home as soon as I could. Nothing else was said and nothing else had to be said. When I arrived at the nursing home, people were all standing around with their heads drooped. Even though I had tried to prepare myself for any bad news when I arrived in his room, seeing several people standing around not looking at me and my father lying in the bed with his bronze, regal, strong face, I completely lost it. I just cried like never before or since. My powerful idol and superhero was gone. He was dead. I have never in my entire life felt so much grief. I fell on top of him and hugged him, vocalizing my deep sorrow and telling him how much I loved him. I let all my emotions out. I think that was good for me.

Neighbors Created a Memorial and Initiated Renaming Street

It should be noted that Reverend Thomas's eulogy at my father's funeral was one of the most powerful and touching ones many of us had ever heard. It caused me and many of my friends and family to experience profound grief and shed many tears.

A few days later I drove to my house in San Pedro while the nursing home was handling my father's arrangements. I saw a huge, beautiful memorial structure that had been erected by all the neighbors on the corner of Gaffey Place and MacArthur Avenue, where my parents' house was located. There was a sign announcing Walter Clements had passed, and there was a beautiful four-by-five-foot picture of him. People were stopping and bringing over memorial flowers, eventually leaving the entire corner filled with flowers.

Memorial forming for Walter Clements

The neighbors decided to launch an effort to give our street MacArthur Avenue a new name: it would be called Walter Clements Avenue in his honor. This started to gain momentum as the family and friends at city hall were behind it. It was moving in the direction to be presented to the city council when my mother spoke up against it, citing the fact that it was creating too much commotion in her life. Nobody asked what that meant, but we eventually dropped the effort.

After he died I did some serious reflection on my relationship with my father and how it impacted me. He had his strengths, as well as his weaknesses, and he had unique qualities. He was generally a serious person. He did not laugh a lot and he was nononsense. There exists the parent who allows three strikes before serious consequences ensue. Not my father. My father was fair, stern, and focused. He did not waste time and expected the same from us. He had somehow instilled a fear of him in us so that we knew we had better do what he said the first time. He wasn't going to have to tell us twice. I long ago blocked the reason I knew I had better do it that way and the reason I feared this kind man, but my brother and I knew Daddy was too busy to waste time repeating himself.

Neither he nor my mom was a cuddly person with us kids. He did not yell at us, nor did he or my mom fight in front of us. Good or bad, this carried over into my personal life. I don't yell at my kids, my wife, or others. Yet one of my downsides is I, like my parents, am not a huggy or cuddly person. I am for the most part quite reserved. As a matter of fact, I remember when I was walking to the tennis courts with one of my good friends in El Segundo, we were having a nice conversation, and as a friendship gesture, he put his arm around my shoulder as we walked. This was so annoying to me, even though I saw him do it often to others. I love my wife, Jean, with all my heart, but she loves to be hugged and cuddled, and I seriously fall short in that area. I will continue to work on this. As my kids have grown older, this flaw has seemed to manifest itself in my interactions with them. I am not perfect but continue to work on it. Fortunately, they seem to exhibit the exact opposite behavior with their own kids.

Chapter 18

Adult Life Experiences

Elected to UCLA Engineering Alumni Board

Around 2004 one of my proudest moments turned into a disaster. I had received my PhD in applied mechanics from UCLA in 1985. I was working at Hughes Aircraft Company and had moved up into middle management. I followed the activities at UCLA but did not really participate in many of them, including the engineering events. Once I went to an engineering function and had a conversation with the president of the UCLA Engineering Alumni Association. We exchanged contact information, and I thought that would be the extent of our interaction. To my surprise, he later contacted me and suggested I apply for a position on the board of the engineering alumni organization. I was honored to be asked and discussed it with Jean. It sounded like an excellent idea, and it would give me a real opportunity to support minority students at the school who may be struggling.

I applied, and I was accepted. I attended my first board meeting on the seventh floor of UCLA's Boelter Hall, where they cordially acknowledged me with little fanfare. I listened carefully as they conducted their business. I quickly related to some of their challenges

UNIVERSITY OF CALIFORNIA, LOS ANGELES   **UCLA**

BERKELEY · DAVIS · IRVINE · LOS ANGELES · RIVERSIDE · SAN DIEGO · SAN FRANCISCO   SANTA BARBARA · SANTA CRUZ

OFFICE OF THE DEAN
SCHOOL OF ENGINEERING AND APPLIED SCIENCE
7400 BOELTER HALL
BOX 951600
LOS ANGELES, CALIFORNIA 90095-1600
(310) 825-2938
FAX (310) 206-4061

April 5, 1999

Dr. Jeffrey Clements
Lab Manager
Engineering Development & Transition
Raytheon Systems Company
P.O. Box 902
Bldg. E1, M/S B115
2000 East Imperial Highway
El Segundo, CA 90245-0902

Dear Dr. Clements:

It is with great pleasure that I congratulate you on your appointment for a two-year term
as an Engineering Alumni Association Governing Board member at the UCLA School
of Engineering and Applied Science.

The Engineering Alumni Association was formed in July 1998 to increase the
involvement of engineering graduates in the School and to support engineering
education and research at UCLA. The inaugural year has been quite successful in
attracting alumni to academic activities and social events.

As a Governing Board member, you play a vital role in the future success of the School
of Engineering and Applied Science. Not only do you represent the voice of
engineering alumni in the School, you are also a representative of the UCLA School of
Engineering and Applied Science within your company and the community.

To that end, we invite you to look for potential relationships and collaborations between
the School and your company, as well as with professional organizations with which you
are affiliated.

I look forward to your involvement in the School and applaud your commitment to
higher education.

Sincerely,

A.R. Frank Wazzan
Dean

and struggles of trying to implement their activities as I had experienced similar challenges during various involvements in other organizations. I felt this was an opportunity for me to make a significant contribution to the association. I mostly listened, but I could not hold back amid the discussion of how to get a document and other literature printed and published. That was when I jumped in and pointed out that I was a manager at Hughes Aircraft, and Hughes would be honored to help UCLA at no cost. I had done some similar things in the past with another organization, and it had not been a problem. There were about twenty-five people in the room, including some professors, but over 80 percent of those present were Asian American students. A professor and I were the only African Americans present. They all turned around and politely listened to my offer of help. To my complete astonishment, they all turned back around and continued their discussion about seeking the means and a source for the printing and publishing of the documents.

I thought to myself that perhaps I had not spoken clearly enough for them to understand what I had offered. Again I listened intently as they resumed their discussion of seeking a source to help with the printing and publishing. I finally thought that I should speak up again and more clearly state my offer. Again they listened, and when I was finished, they impolitely turned their heads to resume the discussion. I was extremely confused and struggled to not jump to conclusions but assumed there was something I was not familiar with or did not understand.

The meeting ended, and I stuck around and managed to briefly chat with Bill. He was busy and thanked me for attending but did not explain why he did not intervene on behalf of my offer. I went home and talked to Jean about the episode. Over the next few months, I attended two more board meetings. Strangely, I experienced very similar behavior from the predominately Asian American attendees in regard to my offers to help. I was so infuriated with their behavior that I felt compelled to lash out at them very disruptively. In general,

I am a very tolerant individual, but I do have an explosive tipping point. I felt I had better leave the meeting before I became completely unprofessional at a minimum or acted like a crazy person. I left and thought long and hard about what action I should take. Wrongly or rightly, I decided to resign and not attend further board meetings. I contacted Bill and resigned, saying it was for personal reasons. That whole incident left me somewhat bitter.

Chaired Hughes Old-Timers Luncheon

Hughes Aircraft employees gather informally for an annual luncheon to socialize and share stories. It began back in the 1970s, and attendance has continued to grow through today. It consists of some of the elite aerospace engineers and scientists, who chat about their activities and the programs they support at Hughes, along with some of the patents they have made. The lunch takes place in November.

During my later years at Hughes, I attended a few of these functions as it was interesting to see some of the older top guys socializing. I eventually became more involved and helped coordinate some of the events. The event has grown larger and larger over time, with over two hundred people in attendance. I had been involved for several years when something surprising occurred. The chairman of the event approached me one day when they were hosting it at the Proud Bird restaurant in El Segundo and asked if I would be willing to be more involved in the planning activities. I thought about it, then said I would be willing to help with whatever was needed. Well, my "whatever was needed" statement brought on a response of major surprise.

Meanwhile, during the course of the banquet, there is usually a five- or ten-minute break for a welcome, then some announcements and statements about the date for next year's banquet and many other activities. Well, the chairperson got up and announced that he had some good news: "Jeff Clements is going to be the new chair." I was sitting at a table and just about fell out of my seat with that surprise announcement. I was not sure if I should jump up and say "No, no, no." I didn't say anything. Everybody started clapping and acknowledging that I was taking over as chairperson. I spoke with the chairman later and told him I was a little surprised, but I could give it a shot. He was grateful and pointed out it was not a big deal. He said I had demonstrated the management and organizational skills desired to make it a success. So I took over and have continued chairing the luncheon for more than six years now. I recruited Judy Neville early to be co-chair and she has been the key to making our reign highly successful over the years. COVID-19 caused us not to gather in 2020 or 2021, but we resumed in 2022. She actually took over the complete reins when I was very restricted during my cancer chemotherapy treatments.

Prior to that I had mixed feelings regarding presiding due to the fact that 98 percent of the attendees are White men and there are only a few brothers in attendance each time. I still wish more Blacks would attend. Only three to four, max, out of nearly two hundred, attend. I still struggle thinking I should exert my energy to help Black people. I have felt that I should focus on helping plan functions for the minorities who are not attending. I still have those concerns. But in any case, I've gotten to know the guys in the group, and they all seem to be fine and supportive, so I'll continue for now, but I still think about trying to help our brothers out in some way.

Best Friend Killed

Life's tragedies can occur at any moment. One occurred in January 2006. I loved to play tennis during the week and with many of my tennis buddies on Saturdays and Sundays. I entered several tennis tournaments and found a good buddy to play with in the doubles matches. His name was Luther Sartor, DDS. He was very bright with an excellent memory and could talk in depth about almost any topic. We argued a lot at first, and I realized he could quote facts and was right most of the time. I settled into not arguing with him and accepted his assessment. The one thing that continued to irritate me was his questioning me on most things I did: Why did I buy that type of tennis bag? Why did I go to dinner at that restaurant? Why did I buy that type of shoe?

Luther and I played in several tournaments. Sometimes we won, and sometimes we lost, but we really enjoyed playing together in either case. He had his own successful dental practice. We were both members of the Kappa Alpha Psi fraternity. He was well liked and very popular in the community. His wife, Gail, was a pharmacist, and they had two kids. They lived in a beautiful house in Ladera Heights. We had a lot of things in common and eventually became best friends.

Luther Sator, Tommy Tucker, Robert Stevenson, and I all were born about the same time, within months of each other. Both Tommy and Luther were prominent dentists in the community. Robert was a Hollywood hairstylist, primarily to the movie star Samuel L. Jackson. When we were all about to turn sixty, we decided to have a joint birthday party. It was absolutely spectacular as we had all our families, friends, and Hollywood celebrities there. People still talk about the party today many years later.

One thing Luther and I would do every Sunday morning for years was play tennis at Centinela Park. I would pick him up from his house, which was about ten blocks from mine, and we would drive

Planning our amazingly successful sixtieth birthday

over to the tennis courts in Inglewood. We did that for many years. One Sunday he told me he was going to go skiing in Mammoth. Even though tennis was his first love, he also loved skiing. This was January 2006. I headed over to his house to pick him up but remembered he said he was going to go skiing so I went ahead directly to the tennis courts. I played with someone else that day. When I got home, my wife told me that she had something to tell me that was unbelievable and very sad. His wife, Gail, had just called and said that Luther had been in a fatal accident in Mammoth.

We immediately went to be with Gail. When we got there, she was in a state of shock and complete disarray. There were about four of us there at the house, and she tried to relay the message she had gotten from someone in Mammoth. They told her he was skiing down the mountain when a whiteout occurred and, skiing alone, he apparently became disoriented and thought he was skiing straight down the hill. In fact, he had turned completely to his left side and headed straight into a mountain, and apparently died instantly. The people that he was skiing with were all waiting for him at the bottom, but since he did not arrive, they went back up to look for him and found him.

The funeral was held at a nearby church, and I was invited to say a few words. I was still devastated by the loss of my best friend and was not able to compose myself to speak. Luther has been gone now for several years, yet I think of him frequently. We remain best friends.

Calbamas Formation

In November 2008 Barack Obama defeated John McCain to become the first African American president of the United States. It is a date that many of us will never forget. It left tears in so many of our eyes to actually see such a major feat accomplished in our lifetime. I was so excited, and I vowed to be at his inauguration in Washington, DC. It turned out that many of my friends had apparently made the same pronouncement in their lives. We talked and all felt we should organize and go as a group. We did, and the Calbamas of California was formed.

We had several meetings in our house to discuss the logistics of where we would stay, where we would go, what we should do, and what events we would attend at the inauguration. It was a very joyous group that mushroomed to over fifty-seven people in number. We made new friendships and firmed up old friendships. We had many prominent people from the community interested in attending, including physicians, doctors, lawyers, judges, engineers, entrepreneurs, businesspeople, housewives, college students, and politicians. Many of the people were from the Ladera Heights community, which was the planning base and where I lived.

I am a native of California, and anything below 60 degrees Fahrenheit is really, really cold. Regrettably, the temperature in Washington, DC, on Obama's inauguration day was an absurd 12 degrees Fahrenheit. My body and mind had no idea what I was doing to them. We stayed in the famous Willard Hotel for the actual inauguration and watched it on TV with lots of folks. Our kids and their friends braved the cold and watched it on the giant field live among the throngs. Jean and I and the kids stayed with Jean's sister in Washington, DC, about eight miles from downtown. Many of the other Calbamas members stayed at or near the Willard Hotel. Inquisitive me did summon the strength to walk around outside the hotel and explore the area

despite all the barricades and police. There were lots of activities taking place.

It was such a wonderful and historic moment; many of us still talk about it. The Obama inauguration and the Calbamas will never be forgotten.

Exposure to Grand Jury Service

In 2013 I began a one-year service with the Los Angeles County Civil Grand Jury. Los Angeles County has a two-tiered grand jury system consisting of the criminal and civil grand jury. The criminal grand jurors serve for three months, while the civil grand jurors serve for one year. I received an invitation in the mail to apply for the grand jury. The invitation implied to me that they only accept the best candidates and not everyone was qualified to be accepted. Only select people, in other words, could join the civil grand jury.

I took this as a challenge to let them know I was more than qualified. Indeed, with my background and all my credentials, I was overqualified. I wanted to let them know that if I wanted to, I could be on their civil grand jury. I completed the application and submitted the paperwork thinking that was as far as I would go. Turns out there were a lot more steps to prove that one was worthy of being on the grand jury, such as security forms, background forms, and so forth. Nevertheless, I continued to follow up on each of their hurdles. Eventually I was required to make an appointment and get approval from a judge after an in-office meeting and an interview to make sure of my qualifications. It turns out my son's buddy's mother was the judge, and I knew her. I figured this would be a slam dunk, and I made an appointment and met with her. I don't know exactly what she submitted from the interview, but I hoped it would go well.

The number of hurdles I had to complete was growing, and I asked myself whether I should continue this arduous process. The next obstacle was a security screening test and fingerprinting and ID process. I made arrangements for that security process and passed it. The final obstacle was to meet in downtown Los Angeles in a courtroom for the final selection. To my surprise, there were one hundred other potential candidates who had made it through the process seeking the grand jury positions. The rules required twenty-three seats to be filled for the civil grand jury. It turned out the final twenty-three were selected by a lottery system. We were randomly assigned numbers from one to one hundred when we entered the room. The administrators began the process, allowing randomly selected numbers to be plucked from a bucket of one hundred ping-pong balls.

They started the process. They selected twenty-two of the twenty-three required. I was certain that I was free and would not be required to serve for one year on this grand jury. Further, I was sort of relieved because I was really questioning whether I wanted to serve for a whole year even though there was decent pay, because it was a

real commitment. Lo and behold, they picked the last number, for the twenty-third juror, and it was mine. I had mixed feelings, but I was grateful that I had qualified. In any case it turned out to be a tremendously rewarding experience to serve on the grand jury for that period. We all bonded after a while. We all came from different professions (e.g., doctors, lawyers, teachers, engineers, admirals, secretaries, priests, etc.).

We did many things together and learned an awful lot about Los Angeles County and its operations. It turns out that the civil grand jury has a lot of power and influence over the activities of the county. We visited jails, hotline centers, the foster care system, youth detention centers, and so forth. We spent the first few weeks getting oriented, learning all about the grand jury system. We received briefings and orientations from the top county officials, who really did an excellent job.

The next step was to form our own committees and identify the areas that we felt should be investigated. Surprisingly there were no significant restrictions or guidelines. We could look at what the previous grand jurors worked on, but we had complete liberty to pursue whatever we felt should be addressed or investigated. We had one year to complete it. There were some standing committees that involved visits to several jails. That was a real eye-opener.

I remember we visited the legendary Twin Towers Jail in downtown Los Angeles. They loaded all of us onto a bus that was labeled "INMATES" and drove us downtown to the jail. We appeared to be in cages riding on the bus, and bystanders looked at us as inmates. When we arrived at the building, the first thing we noticed was the tight security. I thought, *No one could smuggle anything into or out of this jail.* When we got inside, our escorts introduced us to some of the jail protocols and vocabulary (e.g., shot callers, cell bosses). One thing that was really interesting to me was the assignment of colored uniforms based on the offense or circumstance of a given inmate. Drug offenders wore one color, child molesters another color, gays who committed crimes another color, thieves another color, and so forth. There were at least five different colors, I believe. This was necessary to protect each group from the others. Each group resided in a different section of the jail for their own protection. Some inmates with serious mental illnesses were housed in another section of the Twin Towers.

We visited several areas and could see how the staff was managing their section, and we were allowed to ask questions. Some things were very sad and disturbing and left lasting impressions on all of us. The area for gay inmates housed two hundred men, and the interactions there really troubled me. The section for mentally ill inmates had about twenty inmates chained to a sterile aluminum round table also left a lasting, disturbing image with me. Our job was to take notes, discuss our findings, and make sure whatever things we felt were issues were addressed. Ultimately, at the end of our jury service, we had to write a report with all our recommendations and findings, as developed from a completely independent unbiased source—the civil grand jury.

We had many more experiences and undertook many more investigations. We created twenty separate committees; I was on three of them and chaired two. One I chaired was the foster care committee. I learned a lot about the foster care system: how it is handled, how it operates, its shortcomings, its strengths, and its weaknesses. We met and queried the person who oversees the whole foster care system and captured independent feedback from his staff. They gave us candid views on the strengths and weaknesses of the system. We documented our comments, observations, and recommendations in the final iteration of the 2013 Civil Grand Jury Report, available to the public.

Overall, this was a tremendous experience for all of us. We bonded and have continued to hold annual reunions. We were paid about $1,500 per month, including a kind of per diem. Some people joined for the money. I joined to prove to myself that I was qualified to serve. It was an experience I cherish and will never forget.

Personal College Tour and Recognition

In 2015 I received several accolades from various entities, including CSULB. I accepted an invitation to be an engineering contest judge on campus. Just after the judging, the dean of engineering was gracious enough to give me a personal tour of the newest engineering labs, facilities, and projects. I was absolutely mesmerized by and impressed with what he had created. I saw several projects, including drone development and deployment, artificial intelligence development, alternative energy creation schemes, and more. These were not just theoretical projects but actual hardware and working models.

A few months later, I was honored by the NSBE as a guest speaker at CSULB to share my engineering experiences. It was a very nice event as the dean of engineering was there, along with much of his staff, many NSBE members, and some of my family and friends. The event was a lot of fun for me yet emotional at the same time as I was candid about my good and bad experience at CSULB. The event received outstanding coverage by the school paper and the local *Los Angeles Sentinel* newspaper with pictures and a complimentary and compelling story about me, the first Black person to receive a BSME from CSULB.

Jean: The Pillar of Our Family Bonding

Jean has been the pillar that keeps the family meeting together at regular intervals. Jean; my daughter, Malaika; her husband, Ken; their daughters, Ava and Ivy; my son, Austin; his wife, Crystal; and their son, Chase, remain closely bonded with us through Jean's efforts. She has managed to gather these extremely busy adults and kids every Wednesday for a family dinner and for an annual Christmas photo that is sent out in our cards with a write-up about how everyone is progressing in their work and how we are enjoying our time. Everyone's schedules are always tight with events, including homework, late meetings, completing house chores, and so forth. She almost always gets some healthy food, most of it ready-made since she doesn't really like cooking. This helps since each family or family member typically arrives at slightly different times. The grandkids really enjoy seeing each other and playing or creating their own games. One amazing thing is they really enjoy drawing and painting. I have been able to give them a few artistic tips, like what makes a perspective drawing, and they seem to absorb the information. Now, almost every time we get together, they do a little drawing. Their parents point out that they have advanced in art far past their respective classmates. We also share how the parents are progressing in their jobs and careers. Jean conceived of these gatherings during the COVID-19 pandemic, and they continue to this day. We are really blessed to have her.

One day Jean's bonding efforts achieved great rewards. We were all present interacting with each other when Chase, the second-oldest grandchild, said he wanted us to hear what he and Ava had put together. He brought a two-page script with a dialogue for two people. He tried to get our attention as he and Ava started reading the script. Chase is seven and Ava is eight. I was certain their reading skills had not developed well enough to read a script. Anyway, they started reading their respective parts. Ava did not know what a script was. As they proceeded, they read and spoke with clarity and with such realistic expression that it astonished me. I could not believe it. Before I knew it, everyone had stopped their conversations and turned to hear Chase and Ava performing this two-page scene. When they finished, we gave them a resounding standing ovation. Neither their parents nor grandparents had known they could perform like that. We all praised them.

After a few minutes and further discussion, I suggested that one day they should write their own script. All chimed in and agreed. A few minutes later, Chase approached me asking for some paper and a pencil. I gave these items to him and suspected he and Ava were going to try their hand at script writing right then. We all went back to our conversations. It was about time for them to leave since the kids had school the next day. Chase yelled out, "We can't go yet!" because he wanted to enact their script. We were all very surprised they had done something. I insisted on giving them just a few minutes to show us what they had. They announced the title was *A VIP Field Trip*. They began reading the two-person script they had concocted in about twenty minutes. We were all flabbergasted. The grace, harmony, and proper dialogue interaction absolutely blew all of us away.

Jean tries to arrange these family meetings as often as she can to keep some continuity, and I hope she keeps doing it. I certainly appreciate it.

Grandkids performing their own
play they had just created

Current Social Life

Jean and I are not the most socially active people as we enjoy staying at home and just chilling. Here is what I discovered after creating this brief list of our social activities with our friends, colleagues, and family.

We sometimes do things with Norm and tr Langley who live in upper Ladera a few blocks north of us. We go out to lunch or dinner. We sometimes go to their house to socialize with a few other friends. I believe they have one of the most beautiful, elegant houses in Ladera. Norm and I used to go to Bible studies on Thursdays at the West Angeles Church under the leadership of Dr. Hammond. However, when COVID-19 was at its peak, they decided to only have virtual church Bible study. I suspended my attendance until later. I may resume attendance in the near future. Norm's wife tr established a book club consisting of several women from the Ladera community and my wife, Jean, is one of the members. Their interactions seem to be really enjoyable.

Most of the husbands also decided to form a separate book club meeting in between the wives' meetings, but we do not read any books. We just talk and solve most of the world's problems. The men's members are Norman Langley, Greg Delahoussaye, George Tucker, Art Day, and I. We have become good friends and enjoy our men's non-book club.

Jean became a member of the League of Allied Arts (LAA) when Carol Hall was president. The LAA was very active under Carol's leadership and introduced the membership to some amazing affairs and events. Carol was the primary path for me embarking on my new career of fine art.

Jean and I go to a few functions, such as the annual Xmas block club party. We also get together for family functions, such as Thanksgiving and Christmas. We join my brother's family, Sophie, and girls Laura and Tosha and their families; with my family, Jean, Malaika and Ken, Austin and Crystal, and their kids and meet at one of our houses. Norman and tr often join in the family functions. We also enjoy going to Beverly and Dave Kendrix's annual fish fry gatherings. It is an extremely well-organized and well-attended function. I often chat with my ex-neighbor and good friend Michael Lawson, now the head of the Los Angeles Urban League. I was also able to chat with Karen Bass, who is now the mayor of Los Angeles. I was very impressed with her sincerity, honesty, and ambitions at that time.

We used to get together with James and Mary Chitty for a year-end get together with Sandra Willis, Gary and Emelita Johnson, Cliff and Anasa Graves, and a few others. We ended the gatherings because of the COVID-19 restrictions but hope to resume getting together again soon. In the recent past, Jean would organize a group to attend a play or other function. She organized a group of about twenty people to see the play *Hamilton* at the Pantages Theatre in Los Angeles. Until recently, we participated in a group of about ten couples, the Double Ring Club. The members were Ida (president) and Fitzroy Younge, Greg and Yasmin Delahoussaye, Elaine and Wayne Moore, Paulette and Ben Mallard, the Terrys and the Woolfords. It was a religious-based group, but we went to movies and musicals together, and had dinner after most of the functions.

We decided to suspend our membership recently because of my chemotherapy treatment, which was making me less able to get around.

Another annual function Jean and I attend is the 2013 civil grand jury reunion luncheon. Our brilliant jury foreman, Fred Piltz, has been instrumental in hosting the reunion along with Tom Scheerer, Joe DesBarres, Elena Velarde, Mel Widawski, Caroline Kelly, and others. It has been a wonderful gathering, and we enjoy attending the luncheon every year. Typically, we have about half of the original twenty-three members in attendance. I also attend the Hughes Aircraft Company's Old-Timers Lunch held on the first Thursday of every November. It is a four-hour event with about two hundred people in attendance. I am actually the co-chair of the event, and I do enjoy chatting with some of my former colleagues to learn how they are spending retirement.

I am quite impressed and jealous of both Walter and Bill Glass for their latest endeavor involving gardening. Bill was a roommate of ours and also a teammate on our track team at CSULB. After he retired as a highway patrolman, Bill started tinkering with growing vegetables in his backyard. Even though his nickname was farm boy, we did not think he knew much about farming, He got better and better at it and somehow got my brother to start a little garden in his backyard. They both did it because it was relaxing, and it provided a useful product. It turns out they kept expanding, and their gardens became quite extensive. They were able to produce all their vegetables, including squash, cucumbers, tomatoes, greens, lettuce, beets, cantaloupes, watermelons, and more. Walter's wife, Sophie, began to take his vegetable produce and make dinner salads and a few healthy dishes. She became very good at it, and I consider her to have become a very good chef. Now she makes all types of healthy dishes from their expanded garden. We spend time with them, but we don't push them to share their wonderful dishes. However, I am impressed with all of them—Bill, Walt, and Sophie. I consider Sophie to be a master chef, and Walt and Bill are now both farm boys.

I have had to go to Kaiser nearly one time every week for some type of test or evaluation. The tests include X-rays, CT scans, PET scans, blood tests, IVs for chemotherapy, and so forth. These events take up time, but I know I need to continue with them.

The only high-power, high-class social function we attend is the Black Women's Physician Annual Luncheon, as a guest of Dr. Jessie Sherrod. She is always so gracious to get us seats at her table with other prominent professionals from the community. The primary function of the program is to raise money for scholarships for deserving African American females interested in becoming physicians. The functions are always extremely well organized, elegant, and very high class. Dr. Vena Ricketts throws an annual really nice July 4th event that we attend. Additionally, on New Year's Day, I attend the Frank Simmons Tennis Classic organized by Delores Simmons. It is very well attended by the Black tennis community as an annual social function with strong tennis competition.

There is also an occasional funeral we attend.

In compiling and tabulating my social activities, I was stunned to discover that I did not lead a sedentary life akin to my own perception. We generally can be found at home frequently sharing babysitting duties for our grandkids with their other grandparents, Robin and Kenneth (Breeze) Billups.

Success and Failures Fighting Cancer

I have mentioned this before in this memoir that I have had a long battle with prostate cancer. Just to recap, it was first detected in 1994, and I have undergone many treatments through many ups and downs. A key measure of the severity of the cancer is what is known as the PSA. My PSA was relatively low immediately after the surgery. It began to elevate with time. This is not unusual. In fact, many survivors of prostate cancer succumb to the various consequences of the condition marked by elevated PSA readings. The options at the time of my initial treatment were radiation, surgery, or wait and see how things progress. I elected to have the surgery mainly because of the high death rate for prostate cancer, including that of my father, my wife's father, and several others. The death rate for African Americans is significantly higher. Nowadays people are gravitating toward robotic surgery, which is much less invasive and traumatizing to the body.

In any case, I have been on this journey of chemotherapy and hormonal treatments. I have a chart that depicts my various treatments over the last ten or more years that I have undergone. There were six major chemotherapy treatments, in which each lowered my PSA, but after weeks, months, or years, each one failed to continue to keep it at a tolerable level.

It was determined that my cancer had metastasized to the bone, which is a major concern. Metastasis is the leading cause of death. My cancer later began to metastasize and that is where the chemotherapy activity is focused for me. Fortunately, I have little bone pain. Unfortunately, the last effective chemotherapy called Jevtana ceased working for me, and my PSA began to rise. Alarmingly, I have unexpectedly passed out and fallen a few times. Fortunately, no injuries. My friends frequently tell me I have a positive attitude just the way I am. It's not phony or artificial. I am satisfied that at this time I feel fairly well with no significant aches or pains. Additionally, during all this time, there was a new treatment developed that seems to have produced significant successes in the community of prostate cancer survivors. To be eligible to undergo the treatment, one has to meet several criteria. I qualified for the trial treatment. It is a nuclear radiation injection treatment. The treatment kills and/or reduces the cancer cells that might metastasize in my body. I am currently slated to embark on this new treatment at UCLA. I will be going in for consultation in the next weeks. If this works, then I may be back in business and may be around to experience my one hundred and first birthday. Let's keep our fingers crossed. I will.

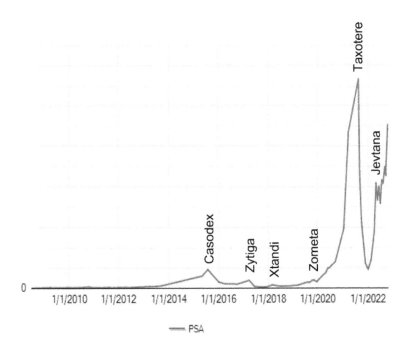

PSA

Appendix

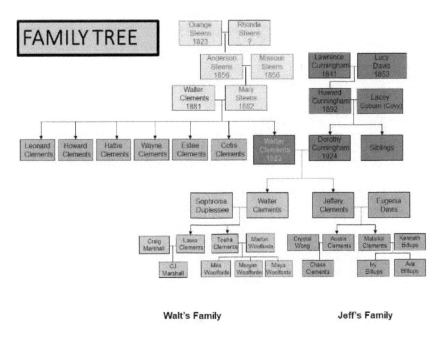

Walt's Family   **Jeff's Family**

Attachment 1: Family Tree

This depicts the most recent version of the Clements family tree. It shows the status of both my brother's family and my family; our kids and grandkids are shown. It also shows my paternal grandfather's family, but it doesn't show much detail about my father's grandfather's side of the family. It does show more detail about my mother's side, with her parents and grandparents. I think this will be updated as time goes on.

Attachment 2: Jeff Clements Family

This photo was taken around 2020. I am at the top center. On my right side is my son-in-law, Ken Billups, and to my left is my son, Austin Clements. Sitting on the left is my daughter, Malaika, holding one of her daughters, Ivy. Next to her is her other daughter, Ava, sitting on the lap of my wife, Eugenia, whom we all call Jean or Gramma. Next to her is Chase Clements, sitting on the lap of his mother, Crystal Clements.

Attachment 3: Clements Family around 2009

My family and my brother's family all got together for this picture along with a few other friends. It includes my mother and father and the one grandchild in existence at that time.

Attachment 4: Clements and Cunningham Families

This is an older photograph, taken in the 1970s, that depicts relatives from both my father's side (Clements) and my mother's side (Cunningham). It was taken in Millington, Tennessee, during a family reunion gathering. A few of my father's sisters are shown, along with a few of my mother's sisters. I do not know any of the young kids or grandkids who are shown in the picture.

Attachment 5: Cunningham Family in Tennessee

This photo was taken in Memphis, Tennessee, around 1960 and depicts several of my mother's sisters and other relatives. She is sitting on the bottom right between two of her sisters; all of them are Cunninghams.

Attachment 6: In Front of Davis Residence

This picture was taken in Atlanta, Georgia, around 2006, on the front steps of the home of Jean's parents, Anderson and Edith Davis. Anderson and Edith are not shown, but a few of their siblings are. Jean and her sister, Ruth, are in the bottom row in the middle. To the right of Jean on the far left of this picture is Austin, and on the far right is Jean's first cousin John Mallett. To his left is my daughter, Malaika. In the background are some other friends and family from California, Italy, Mississippi, Georgia, and South Carolina.

Attachment 7: Jean's Family Attending Swearing In

This photo was taken around 1992 in Washington, DC, during Ruth's inauguration as an ambassador. Shown primarily are the Davis family, including Anderson and Edith Davis, along with Ruth, Jean, the kids, Austin and Malaika, and me. The photo also includes a few of Jean's mother's sisters and a few other relatives.

Attachment 8: Centinela Tennis Buddies 1

This is a picture of some of my tennis hacker buddies; we play regularly on Sunday mornings at Centinela Park in Inglewood. We primarily play doubles matches. Some of the guys are good, and all are extremely competitive. We have been doing this for years and enjoy each other's company. We frequently socialize outside of tennis and have remained good friends over the years.

Tennis 2

Attachment 9: Centinela Tennis Buddies 2 ~ 2018

This picture is of the same group of tennis players on a different day at the same park in Inglewood but includes some who did not appear in the previous photo.

Attachment 10: Barack Obama Inauguration

President Barack Obama was inaugurated on January 20, 2009. This is a picture of a portion of the group that went to Washington, DC, to witness the inauguration. We were meeting in my living room to discuss our travel plans and itinerary. The group included die-hard Barack Obama supporters, friends, and some community leaders. We had a wonderful time planning the event and making arrangements to be there and attend many of the functions. It was a phenomenally successful adventure.

Ingram Content Group UK Ltd.
Milton Keynes UK
UKHW020033040523
421194UK00021B/192/J